Fast and Simple Steps to Profit from Trend Trading

Learn to Make Money in Bull and Bear Markets

Master the Basics of Fundamental and Technical Analysis

Henry Ong

Fast and Simple Steps to Profit from Trend Trading
Published by
Roc Holdings Pte Ltd
www.TrendTradingSignalSystem.com

Acknowledgement: I would like to thank StockCharts.com for providing excellent free charts.

This book is dedicated to my parents and my loving wife who have to put up with the countless nights that I stayed up to finish this book.

About the Author

Henry Ong has accumulated many years of practical trading experience. He has held senior positions in various international firms and advised corporations and wealthy individuals regarding finance, investments, trading, mergers & acquisitions and complex deal structuring. He enjoys sharing his knowledge in financial, trading, investment and business subjects. From his experience, he believes a simple step-by-step guide is highly effective in guiding most beginners. This led him to write this book which aims to provide readers with seven simple steps on how to become a successful trend trader. Henry graduated from Cornell University and is also a Chartered Public Accountant and Chartered Financial Analyst.

Fast and Simple Contents

Fast And Simple Steps To Profit From Trend Trading

Fast And Simple Steps To Profit From Trend Trading

Introduction

What is trend trading?

Trend trading is a trading strategy that tries to take advantage of the up and down trends of securities. Trend traders typically try to use technical and fundamental analysis to identify trends as early as possible so that they can profit from them. The trends can be short to long term trends depending on the trader's preferences and objectives.

Does trend trading work?

"Buy and hold" investing strategy does not seem to work well over the past 15 years. A "buy and hold" investor of the S&P500 index will incur a 7% loss from end of 1997 to 2008 while a trader that follows the major trends will make about 560% return or about 19% annual return during the same period!

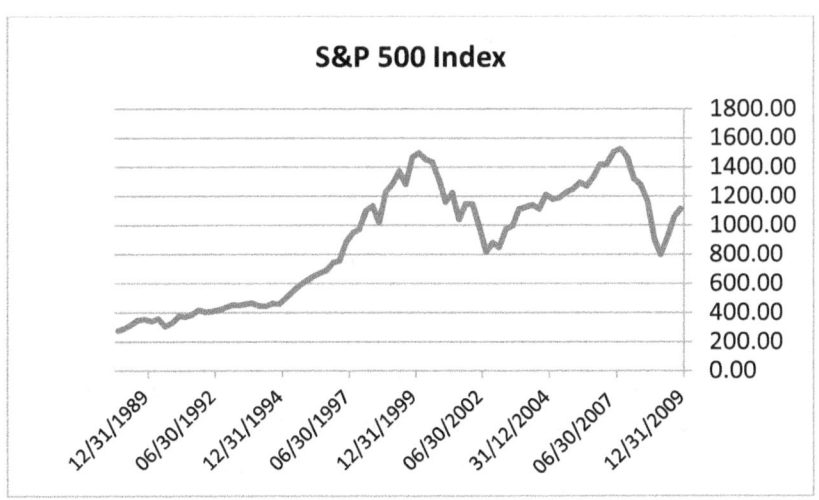

Figure 1-1: S&P 500 Index chart

As you can see from the Figure 1-1, the S&P 500 index had undergone two major bull and bear markets from 1997 to 2008. In our example, the long term investor who bought the index in 1997 will only breakeven in 2009!

However, assuming if you are to carry out the trend following trades during this period as described in Figure 1-2, your $10,000 will turn into $66,350 compared to $9400 if you are to employ "buy and hold" strategy. That is equivalent to multiplying your money more than 5.6 times or almost 19% per annum! Of course, you might not be able to time the tops and bottoms so accurately, but if you master trend trading, you will definitely perform much better than just employing a "buy-and-hold" strategy in this instance.

Entry Date	Index	Order	Return[1]	Exit Value
31 Dec 1997	970.43	Buy	57.4%	$15,700
24 Mar 2000	1527.46	Short Sell	49.1%	$23,410
9 Oct 2002	776.76	Buy	99.9%	$46,790
19 Jul 2007	1553.08	Short Sell	41.8%	$66,350
31 Dec 2008[2]	903.25	Close Short	NA	

1: Content in table above excludes dividends earned or paid, so actual returns most likely will be higher.
2. Exit on 31 Dec 2008 for 19 Jul 07 short sell order is used for simplicity, if you hold till 9 Mar 2009 when S&P 500 is at 676, you would have made more.

Figure 1-2: Returns from trend trading S&P 500 Index from 31 Dec 1997 to 31 Dec 2008

You might think 19% annual return is not exciting but if you compound 19% over a period of 30 years, your $10,000 will grow to $1.85 million in 30 years time! That is 185 times your initial capital! A record that even Warren Buffet will be proud of. And this is just the S&P 500 index!

Contrary to popular belief, Warren Buffet is not just a "buy and hold" investor. Buffet started out as perhaps one of the most sophisticated securities trader and hedge fund manager in the world. For example he practiced highly sophisticated arbitrage trading. Buffet did mention that he kept his personal investments and trading apart from Berkshire. One of the key reasons Buffet held a large part of Berkshire's investments for a long time in the later part of his career is because Berkshire owns huge stakes in its portfolio companies and it simply cannot trade their shares in the markets like most of us do.

Hence, whatever your trading or investment philosophy is, trend trading is an important and powerful tool that you should include in your repertoire of skills.

Objectives of this book

This book is meant to be a guide to help you succeed in making consistent profits from trend trading regardless of the direction of the market. But to be successful in trend trading, you need pre-requisite knowledge and skills. But I understand that you have limited time to learn those knowledge and skills.

Hence, this a straightforward guide book that aims to help you learn trend trading quickly by providing you with step-by-step guide that will enable you to:

✓ Learn the basics of trend trading;

✓ Set up a trend trading system;

✓ Improve technical analysis or fundamental analysis skills;

✓ Improve your trading techniques, system or results; and

✓ Start trend trading with minimal prior knowledge.

To help you achieve these objectives, this book will describe 7 simple steps that you can complete within 3 days of diligent work. There is an Action List at the end of each step for you to complete. Under each task in the Action List, there may be tips and guides to help you complete each task.

If you are new to trend trading and you really want to be a successful trend trader, you should complete the tasks in all the Action Lists. For those who are experienced trend traders, you may go to the sections that interest you.

If you diligently complete the actions required in the Action Lists and master the important lessons in this book, you will be a very successful trader of stocks, Exchange Traded Funds ("ETFs") and even foreign exchange (or "forex" for short).

However, your trend trading education should not end here. You need to reference other books or even visit our website to further improve your trading knowledge and skills.

Seven Fast and Simple Steps to Trend Trading Success

The seven steps that are described in this book should help new traders master the basics of trend trading quickly and easily. Hence, I suggest that you go through these steps in chronological order.

The seven steps to help you master trend trading basics are:

1. Resolve to increase your wealth from trading

2. Understand your risk appetite and personality

3. Increase your awareness of trading opportunities

4. Learn technical and fundamental analysis

5. Master different order types

6. Develop your trend trading strategy and system

7. Review and fine tune your goals and system

No one can guarantee that you will make money in every trade, as that is simply impossible. Even great investors and traders such as Warren Buffet make mistakes in some of their trades and investments. Hence, don't be discouraged if some of your trades are unsuccessful.

With a proper trend trading system that you will learn to build here, you will be able to use your mistakes to help you improve your system and increase your future trading profits! A trader with a good system will definitely be more successful than the trader without one.

Let the Journey Begin

Enough said, as I want to make this book a fast and simple read.

Do try to take notes and carry out the actions required of you in the Action Lists. You can visit *www.trendtradingsignalsystem.com* for more resources, trading tips and some sample templates for the tasks in the Action Lists.

Good luck and enjoy the journey!

Step 1 - Resolve to increase your wealth from trading

Do you really want to make money from trading?

I believe your answer is "Yes" else you won't be reading this book. But wanting to make money from trading is not enough, you need a burning desire to make money from trading.

Hence, the most important step is to ask yourself whether you want to increase your wealth through trading. If so, you will learn in this book fast and simple steps that will help you increase your wealth from trend trading.

What I am talking about here is not day trading which basically refers to traders who sit in front of their computers everyday when the market opens to trade stocks based on intraday movements. In my view, this is not a good way to increase your wealth for most people as it probably destroys your health before it increases your wealth. There are successful day traders out there but they are a small minority as most people cannot afford the time for day trading.

However, trend trading by our definition will allow you enough time to enjoy other things that life offers but still make you loads of money when you are away from trading desk! There are many types of trend trading as people have different trading styles. You have to find yours. For example, some prefer to trade daily while there are others who prefer to look at charts only once a week.

This book does not advocate a particular style as you really have to find the style that suits your personality, character, time, capital resources, returns expectations and risk appetite. It is highly important that you find a trading style that suits you and stick to it. This book will cover the various trading styles later.

A strong resolve to make money from trading ETFs and stocks is critical as people with weak desire usually give up easily after they encounter some setbacks.

Persistence and diligence are crucial in the trading business, that's why you really need to convince yourself that you want to do this. Even following the simple instructions in this book requires persistence and diligence.

Why master trend trading?

In order to have strong resolve, you need to be absolutely convinced about the benefits of trend trading. Hence, some key benefits of trend trading are listed below for your reference:

- **Put your money to work** – money deposited in savings accounts hardly earn any significant interest from banks nowadays. Furthermore, banks will almost always pay you interest rates that are lower than inflation rate. So you are losing money just by putting money in the bank. Whereas a good trend trader should expect to earn above the stock market index return which historically was about 10% per year. Besides, stock prices generally rise with inflation. Hence, making trend trading a reasonably good hedge against inflation.

- **Make money regardless of price direction** – Worried about bear market? With trend trading, you should look at bear market as a money making opportunity, just like a bull market, because good trend traders make money whether the market is up or down. The price direction of the security doesn't matter to them as long as they can establish a trend is in place. Just remember "The Trend Is Your Friend" when it comes to trend trading. Trend traders simply buy when the price is trending upwards and short sell or buy put options when the price is trending down. As long as traders know the price direction of the products that they are trading, they can make significant profits.

- **Time flexibility** – With today's interconnectivity, you can trade almost any time of the day as market opening times of American, European and Asian exchanges overlap. So even if you have a day job, you can find time after work to analyze and trade.

- **Location independence** – you can trade at home, at work (not that you should or need to spend much of your working hours trading), during vacations and now even on the go. So you can increase your wealth anywhere in the world as long as you are connected to your broker.

- **Free up your time** – if you focus only on high probability trades and big stories then you do not need to spend hours analyzing ETFs and stocks. With increasing popularity and proliferation of ETFs, it has made trend trading even less time consuming as ETFs typically require less complicated fundamental analysis. Furthermore, with a sound trend trading system, your trend trading should become more mechanical, saving you precious time.

- **Earn while you sleep** – your trading portfolio can help you make money while you are away. The key to making outsized profits is from analyzing the opportunity before pulling the trigger to trade. Not staring at the trading screen. Of course, prices can move against you and you might lose some money but with proper risk management system in place, any loss should be manageable and you can take part in the market another time.

- **Little capital needed** – some people have the wrong impression that they need to have at least hundreds of thousands of dollars to trade. This cannot be further away from the truth. Regulators in the USA have imposed $25,000 minimum equity limit for day traders but if you are not a day trader, you do not need that amount of capital. Furthermore, many brokerages nowadays offer leverage – but do use margin (equivalent to your brokerage lending you money) with care. Trading is perhaps one of the least capital intensive business that a person can start. For as little as a few thousand dollars, you can be on your way to be a part-time trader especially if you use many of the discount brokerages out there that charges very low fees. That said, the amount of capital does influence the absolute amount of profits you can make. For those who do not have multi-million dollar trading capital, you can do well do by limiting the number of positions you have. Furthermore, there are many free applications available to help you screen for trading opportunities.

- **Low cost** – trading commissions are a direct cost of trading. We are fortunate to live in the digital age whereby there are numerous discount brokers that will enable you to trade ETFs, stocks, foreign exchange, commodities, etc at such low or even no fees. For most people, the costs you need to incur for trading are:

  o a computer - which most of us have anyway
  o a mobile phone – needed only if you need to trade on the move

- o internet connection - good broadband connectivity is necessary
- o books – you need to learn about trading, technical and fundamental analysis
- o brokerage – there are many discount brokers. Refer to our website for some of them
- o online newsletters and trading systems subscriptions, some of the news subscriptions are free
- o continuous training and education – new events, trends, more advanced trading techniques and new applications are being invented all the time so it is important that you keep yourself updated

Action List for Step 1

1. List down the reasons that inspire you to embark on trend trading on your "Dream List". Set a profit target for yourself and dream of what you can achieve if you become a successful trend trader.

2. Stick a copy of your *"Dream List"* on the wall right in front of the computer that you use to trade with.

TIP: Every time you feel like giving up, take a look at the Dream List, close your eyes and keep repeating the reasons you stated in the list in your head. Do it at least 3 times. You will find yourself reenergized again!

Notes for Step 1

Step 2 - Understand your risk appetite

This might sound cliché to many people but knowing your risk appetite is extremely important in trading. If you don't know your risk appetite, then you won't know the right amount of capital to commit to your trading venture and for each trade.

Some traders lose sleep over their open trade positions. This is absolutely unnecessary! If you are losing sleep over your open trading positions then you most likely are risking too much capital for your own good. You should review the amount of risk you are undertaking.

If you are new to trading, start small. Don't risk everything that you have got or you might panic and commit silly mistakes.

Steps to determine your risk appetite

The steps stated below help you to better understand your risk appetite.

1) **Know how much capital you can afford:** Set aside your minimum emergency fund. No one has the same needs so there is no magic formula. A popular advice given is that one should have emergency funds for at least six months of expenses. However, each person has his own sets of issues to deal with. Hence, covering six months of expenses might be too much or too little for you. Talk to your financial advisor if you are in doubt. If your gut tells you that you are risking too much, then you should listen to your gut and cut back. Reduce the capital you use for trading in such a case and top up your trading capital at a later time.

2) **Know your support network**: If you have strong financial support from family and friends then perhaps you can take more risk than someone who does not have family or friends to fall back on. However, your support network is really your last resort and it should never be abused. Never ever risk so much capital in trading that you have to rely on others to pay your trading debts.

3) **Determine your income lifecycle:** Income lifecycle starts from the time you can start earning income till the day you leave this world. Income includes passive income like dividends and interests. Hence, at each stage of your life, the amount you earn, your income source and potential to earn future income may be different. For example, a typical young person who just graduated from school might earn less than someone in the same field who has twenty years of work experience but the younger person might have higher income potential since he has a longer road ahead of him. While a retiree who no longer draws wages will find it very hard to recover once he loses all his capital. Hence, a person with less income potential should not risk all his capital in risky trades.

4) **Personality:** Some people can take a lot of risk without losing any sleep while others cannot stand losing a dime in any form of investments even if it is only paper loss. Personality plays a huge part in a person's willingness to take risks and ability to handle risks. It also plays an important role in determining your trading style. If you feel very anxious that your trade positions remain open at the end of the trading day, then you should consider whether you are risking too much capital or you must close all your positions at the end of each day. You will get to know your "trading" personality better after some trades. Hence, you might need to adjust your trading system as you get to know yourself better.

5) **Other short term demands for your capital**: You should seriously consider setting aside money that you need to spend in the near future, for example within 3 to 6 months, and not use it for trading. For example, if you absolutely need to use $50,000 to buy a house to live in within 3 months then you should try not to use that $50,000 in trading. It is not just that you are risking too much, putting money that you need in the near future could adversely affect your trading results as you might act irrationally.

TIP: Statistics taught us that any event that has even a very small probability of happening will eventually happen – it is just a matter of time. Hence, never get greedy or complacent even when you become a successful trader. Many traders fail most miserably because of complacency - ask Lehman Brothers and Merrill Lynch bankers. When you think you are becoming a gambler or you have a sequence of bad trades, then you should take a break from trading for a while to sort out your emotions.

Action List for Step 2

1) Determine your emergency fund amount by taking your expenditures and multiply it by at least 6 times.

   My emergency fund = _____

2) Determine your short term spending needs by listing out big ticket items that you need to spend on within the next six months. You should do not use the money you need in the short term for trading. But if you still want to use it then you should definitely not use it to trade highly leveraged products such as foreign exchange with high leverage or options.

Big Ticket Item	Amount

3) Tally how much cash you have and deduct that with your required emergency fund and short term spending needs. That will be the maximum amount of trading capital you have. Remember to consider your liabilities as well.

Total Cash   =

Minus Emergency Funds   =

Minus Short Term Spending Needs   =

_____

Available Funds for Trading   =

4) Ask yourself if you need any of your family members or friends to help you if you lose most or even all your trading capital. If you seriously think you will need their support in such an event, then you might have put too much capital into trading! Reduce it.

Answer: YES / NO

5) List down all your alternative sources of income.

    1. _____

    2. _____

    3. _____

    4. _____

    5. _____

6) Write down as many potential employment opportunities as possible. This list will hopefully help to calm your nerves when the going gets tough.

_____

_____

_____

7) Are you a gambler? If you are a gambler then you should really be really extra careful with risk management. Be frank to yourself here as it will only do you good. Trading is a business and it is not gambling. Try to find a partner or mentor to ensure that you do not over leverage. Do not trade products of mass destruction, such as foreign exchange and derivatives, until you are successful with trading stocks and ETFs with minimal leverage. Even when you are successful, you should not risk more than 20 percent of your capital in trading leveraged products.

8) Ask yourself if you prefer to make many small profits and losses within a short time period or you prefer to hold your position for longer period of time. Some traders combine different trading styles which is fine as well.

    A. Small profits/loss and short holding period
    B. Potential for larger profits/loss per trade and longer holding period

    Select one of the above.

9) A list of trading styles is provided below so that you can decide which style suits your personality and objectives better.

Day Trading

- Holds position for a few minutes to a few hours.
- Closes all positions before the end of each trading day.
- Uses high leverage most of the time to so as to magnify small gains from intraday movements.

Personality: Strongly desires instant results. Likely to be introverts who work in front of computers for no less than 10 hours every day. Ability to detach emotions from results and react very quickly to changes. Likes to read charts and does not like to analyze fundamentals too much. Prefers to trade highly liquid and at times leveraged financial instruments.

Swing trading or short term trend trading

- Relies on more on short term trends and chart patterns rather than fundamentals.
- Takes advantage of price movements that happens over a few days to a few weeks.
- Significant amount of leverage might be used. Some traders might trade derivatives such as options.

Personality: Wants fast results but are usually slightly more patient than day traders. Has the time to spend a few hours daily to analyze portfolio and trading opportunities. Possesses some fundamental analysis skills but relies more on technical analysis.

Medium term trend trading or position traders

- Bases decision on fundamental analysis and technical analysis.
- Uses technical analysis to signal entry and exit points.
- Uses leverage selectively.
- Holds positions for weeks or months if stop orders are not triggered. Usually uses less leverage than swing traders.

Personality: Rather patient and willing to wait weeks or even months before banking in profits. Usually relies on fundamental analysis to support trading decisions. Uses technical analysis to find entry and exit points. Not able or willing to trade daily.

Long term trend trading

- Relies more on fundamental analysis and might use technical analysis to signal entry and exit points.
- Makes trading decisions based on economic cycles, which means holding position for over a year is common.
- Uses little or no leverage in trading.

Personality: Not easily influenced by even major pullbacks and corrections as long as the general trend remains the same. Willing to wait months or even years before banking in profits. Not willing to analyze portfolio and opportunities on a daily or even weekly basis. Only willing to make changes to portfolio when convinced that long term fundamentals are going to change soon or have changed.

My Preferred Trading Style is: _____

Notes for Step 2

Step 3 – Increase your awareness of opportunities

Identify opportunities from your daily life

New information is important for finding the right product to trend trade and for determining the direction of the trend. Information if used wisely translates into profits in trading. When reading news, try to analyze how the news will affect various sectors, industries and corporations. Try to act on the new information as soon as you form a solid opinion based on sound analysis. It is really not that difficult to know the direction of a trend with some practice.

Besides reading articles, the things that we come into contact with in our daily activities give us extremely helpful clues as to whether certain sectors, industries or companies will do well or badly. For example, when many consumers started buying iPhone instead of Nokia's higher end models from 2008, you can reasonably conclude that Apple's share price will appreciate in value from 2008, while Nokia and Motorola are going to suffer declines in profits.

Similarly, when you notice Starbucks is rapidly opening new outlets in your city a decade ago, you probably can deduce this is a new lifestyle trend and you should take a closer look at Starbucks' stock back then.

TIP: Stock prices feed on news. You must learn to decipher news that have long term impact and those that have only short term impact on stock prices. Usually several pieces of news will be made public before a big shift in long term trend takes place. Hence, there are usually ample warning signs and some of the best warning signs can easily be observed from our daily activities.

For example, prior to the big stock market crash in September 2008, there are already signs of a huge bear market looming. In the middle of 2007, the S&P 500 index made a few outsized corrections. After that, Bear Stearns collapsed in March 2008, a good half year before Lehman Brothers collapsed. Furthermore, the housing market in the US has been in a slump since 2007. If you pay attention to all these warning signs prior to September 2008 then you might have saved yourself a lot of money and perhaps even make some in the process by shorting stocks.

Key indicators to look out for

It is highly important to observe and analyze the pieces of information that you can glean from your daily life. Key indicators to look out for include:

- **GDP** – GDP figures are reported monthly in the US. You can easily judge GDP trends by talking to people, observing the number of shoppers in malls, general spending mood, etc. Such daily observations often act as leading or confirming indicators regarding the direction of GDP change.

- **Inflation** – this can be observed from the food you buy, the transport prices you pay, rental and housing prices and energy prices as these are major components of the Consumer Price Index (CPI) that the government releases to the public. If inflation starts recovering, it is time to enter the market and if it begins to overheat the central bank will usually start to increase interest rates.

- **Interest rates** – the stock market recovery usually starts when the interest rates are at its historic recent lows, i.e. after a series of interest rates reduction. When the central bank starts raising interest rates, the bull market is usually at its full swing. You can usually expect the market to go south before the central bank completes its interest raising spree.

- **Consumer confidence** – when consumer confidence is at all time high, it is time to consider trimming long positions in your trade. When consumer confidence is at all time low, prepare enough capital to enter the stock market.

TIP: The trends of the four indicators mentioned above are usually more important than their absolute values. For example, observe if inflation rate is trending above the government's target inflation rate, then the government will usually introduce economy cooling measures to control inflation rate.

Be observant because it will help you make a much better trend trader.

Action List for Step 3

1) Subscribe to your local newspapers. If you are really serious about trading, subscribe to Wall Street Journal or other business news providers. Make it a habit to read the newspapers before the market opens every day.

2) There are many online business news providers such as Yahoo Finance, Google Finance and MarketWatch, make sure you set at least one of them to be your browser's home page if you are serious about trading. It is even better that you have several of

these financial/ business websites set as your home pages of your internet browser.

List the online news providers that you have set as your internet browser home page:

1. _____
2. _____
3. _____
4. _____

3) If you want to focus on a particular industry or country then subscribe to online trade journals or other industry publications online. There are many free publications that are available online, simply do a search with the help of any popular search engine using the industry name and "publication" or "journal" as your search keywords. Bookmark all of them in an organized fashion by classifying the different news sources.

The industry/country print or online publications that I have found or subscribed are:

1. _____
2. _____
3. _____
4. _____
5. _____
6. _____

4) Start observing key products and services that you and your family are using every day and determine if they are becoming more or less popular, or whether they are getting better or worse. If you have a strong gut feel that a product or service is catching on or being phased out, go on the web to check out which company produced it and analyze how the company is doing. List down the products and service and your corresponding observations in the table below or use the notes page at the end of the chapter.

Product / Service	Observations

5) Find out the companies behind all the products and services listed in the table above. Next, determine whether any of the companies you have identified are publicly listed.

1. _____

2. _____

3. _____

4. _____

Note: Most cellular phones come with notepad application nowadays so you do not need to carry a notepad around anymore to jot down ideas.

6) Start listening to the official messages from the Federal Reserve and ask yourself what impact their statements will have on the S&P 500 index. Determine whether your earlier analysis is correct a week after the announcement of the latest FOMC meeting minutes by comparing your analysis to the actual movements of the S&P 500 index. Do this for at least one month before you start trading.

Next FOMC meeting minutes release date is _____.

Likely Impact of FOMC statement on S&P 500 is Bullish / Bearish (select one).

After 5 trading days, ask yourself if your above conclusion is correct.

Notes for Step 3

_____

_____

_____

_____

_____

_____

_____

_____

_____

_____

_____

_____

_____

_____

_____

Step 4 – Learn Technical and Fundamental Analysis

You need to master technical and fundamental analysis to do well in trend trading because fundamental analysis helps you determine the rationale behind the price movements over the longer term, while technical analysis is useful in determining when to put in your buy and sell orders.

You will do much better if you do not go against the conclusions that you have drawn from your fundamental or technical analysis. You should only put in an order if technical analysis and fundamental analysis provide the same conclusion. You should not bend this rule as you might profit in the short term but over the long run you will find it extremely challenging to consistently profit from trend trading.

Fundamental analysis and technical analysis are extensively covered in many books dedicated to each topic. The fundamental analysis and technical analysis basics that are covered in this book should be sufficient for you to begin your trend trading journey as these are the key skills needed for you to be able to pick out the major trends from the noise in the markets.

There are many successful trend traders who swear by technical analysis only. However, most successful trend traders do consciously consider the underlying drivers of price movements before they place a trade. That's why most successful trend traders focus on certain instruments so that they can better understand the products that they are trading.

Basics of Fundamental Analysis

Figure out the economic cycle

This is perhaps the most important first step. Ask yourself whether the economy is on its way up or on its way down over the next year. Determining economic cycles will help you immensely in making medium to long term trading decisions even if you might not be able to time the top and bottom of stock market cycles.

An economic cycle basically consists of 4 stages as explained below:

1. **The Peak** – characterized by high Federal Funds Rates, increasing inflation, very high consumer confidence, decreasing unemployment and escalating asset prices. If left uncontrolled, it might lead to a bubble.

2. **The Recession** – when the good times end, it often ends with a bang. Usually it is caused by rapid loss of confidence by investors and consumers resulting in rapidly decreasing asset prices, escalating inventories, increasing unemployment or other issues. The Federal Reserve usually starts to cut interest rates.

3. **The Trough** – Bottoming of the recession is called a trough. Usually unemployment rate reaches a recent high and all the indicators points to the worst possible outcome. Asset prices start to bottom out and stop decreasing rapidly if at all. Money supply tends to have increased a lot to help stabilize prices.

4. **The Recovery and Expansion** – when asset prices are very cheap, investors will start buying them. It happens when the government's actions to boost the economy begins to take

effect. Confidence starts returning and investments increase. That is when leading indicators start to point upwards.

To help determine the economic cycle before the National Bureau of Economic Research ("NBER") announces it because there are usually lagging, there are usually a few indicators you can use.

- **Leading Economic Index** published monthly by the Conference Board. If the index begins to move downwards, then there is a strong possibility that the economy is in decline. Many components such as money flow, interest rate spread and weekly manufacturing hours make up the Leading Economic Index, you can get a copy of the report from the Conference Board to read the details. Pay special attention to its release.

- **Federal Funds Rate** ("Fed Rate" or commonly known as "interest rates") is the rate that banks charge each other for overnight loans of federal funds, which are the reserves held by banks at the Federal Reserve (the "Fed"). The general signal is that the market is typically bearish when the Fed is cutting Fed Rate as it needs to lower interest rates to revitalize a flagging economy. The economy tends to start recovering when the Fed Rate is held steady at a very low rate. It is important to remember that the stock market tends to recover slightly ahead of the economy. When the Fed Rate is increasing again, the bull market is usually in its full swing and the Fed is trying to prevent the economy from overheating. You can begin to trim your long positions at the later stages of interest rate increases.

- **Consumer Sentiment Index** published by University of Michigan and **Consumer Confidence Index** published by the Conference Board are popular indicators of consumer confidence in the US. They might fluctuate from month to month and they might lag stock market price movements but the trends of these two indices are important for determining the general economic cycle. Positive surprises are typically good news for stock market and vice versa.

- **Change in GDP** which is published by the BEA, is a useful but lagging indicator of the stock market trends. The direction and momentum of GDP growth are perhaps more important than its absolute value in trend trading.

- **Foreign exchange movements** are important considerations in trend trading. If US economy is stronger than the other country in the currency pair then US dollar tends to appreciate and vice versa. For example, if the European Union's economy is growing more strongly than the US, then the euro is likely to strengthen against the US dollar. If US currency depreciates rapidly, it might not bode well for US stocks as investors may be less willing to hold on to assets denominated in US dollars. However, there are many forces at play when it comes to foreign exchange movement. In general, capital flocks to where foreign exchange rates tend to increase in comparison to the investor's domestic currency.

- **Inflation rate** is critical as it influences the Fed's decision on the Fed Rate. Rapidly increasing inflation is a sign of overheating economy and you need to be more alert as the Fed is likely to increase the Fed Rate to reign in on inflation.

- **S&P 500 Index and Volatility index** ("VIX") are important indices that you should monitor closely. If the VIX is increasing over a period of time, then there is fear in the market. If the bullish market makes volatile price movements, the bullish trend might be ending. The direction of the S&P 500 Index will help confirm this. That is why using both fundamental analysis and technical analysis is important. However, the volatility index is itself very volatile. Hence it is better to use its 20-day moving average to help determine if it is trending upwards or downwards.

TIP: Always monitor the monitor the general direction of stock market indices like S&P 500 index and volatility index before you decide to trade on any ETF and stock.

Sector Analysis and Rotation

As the economy goes through bull and bear markets, certain sectors will perform better than others at different times. The popularity of trading and investing in sector tracking ETFs have increased in recent times due to their relatively higher liquidity and lower volatility than most stocks. Especially popular are the Sector Select SPDR ETFs which track nine key sectors in the US economy. The nine ETFs are:

1. Consumer Discretionary (Symbol: XLY)
2. Consumer Staples (Symbol: XLP)
3. Energy (Symbol: XLE)
4. Financial (Symbol: XLF)
5. Healthcare (Symbol: XLV)
6. Industrial (Symbol: XLI)
7. Materials (Symbol: XLB)
8. Technology (Symbol: XLK)
9. Utilities (Symbol: XLU)

To determine which sector to trade in is important as the demise of certain key sectors such as financial sector will have important implications to other sectors in a relatively short space of time. Whereas increasing profits of companies in the Materials and Energy sectors may help propel the stock market to new highs but it could lead to high inflation and the eventual fall of the market if inflation goes out of hand.

TIP: Pay close attention to all sectors and pick individual winners within the sector to boost your returns. For example, in a bull market driven by technology sector, you might want to buy one or two stocks that you think have the best price increase potential in this sector to help you beat the sector index. However, do this only when you become an expert of that sector.

Sectors	Drivers / Indicators
Consumer discretionary (XLY) – covers automobiles, entertainment, luxury goods, restaurants, etc.	• GDP Growth – If the economy is generally improving or doing well, consumer discretionary spending will increase and vice versa. • GDP (PPP) per capital – If GDP per capital measured in PPP terms is increasing then consumers can afford more goods and services which will usually spur the growth of discretionary products. • Real earnings growth – if real earnings increase, consumers have more disposable income to spend on discretionary

Sectors	Drivers / Indicators

products.

- Unemployment level –more people can spend on discretionary products when unemployment level is low. High or increasing unemployment levels will negatively affect consumer sentiment.

- Consumer confidence/sentiment index – if consumers are more confident about the future, they tend to spend more on discretionary items especially the more expensive items such as automobiles and luxury goods are sensitive to this measure.

- Interest rates – a lot of consumer discretionary items such as automobiles and more expensive electronics goods might be bought using loans. Consumers will be weary of purchasing expensive products if credit is more expensive.

- Inflation rate –Basic material price increases might soon lead to more expensive consumer products such as autos. Hence, if inflation rate exceeds acceptable region, profits of companies in this sector may be adversely affected.

Sectors	Drivers / Indicators
Consumer Staples (XLP) – covers food & beverage, discount and grocery stores, etc.	• Population growth – consumption of staples is quite stable for a relatively wealthy country. A growing population means more staple goods and services will be consumed. • GDP (PPP) per capita growth – for a developed country like USA, this measure might not influence staples consumption as much as a developing country as staples consumption is relatively stable above a certain income level. • Unemployment level – only critical if unemployment rate is at a high level and for a prolonged period of time. Companies focused on domestic consumption will typically do poorly if unemployment level remains high for an extended period of time. • Raw material prices – rapid and significant increase in raw material prices will adversely affect the profits of staple goods manufacturers as often they are not able to pass on the increased costs quickly and fully to retailers and consumers.

Sectors	Drivers / Indicators
Energy (XLE) – crude oil and natural gas producers, and drilling companies and other energy-related services.	• GDP growth – a growing economy will consume more energy. If capacity is not able to meet demand, it might lead to higher energy prices which will increase profits of energy companies. • Crude oil prices – higher crude oil prices usually translate to higher profits for oil majors that make up the bulk of the ETF holdings because they usually can pass on all if not most of the increased costs to their customers. • Oil inventory –higher oil inventory will impact oil prices negatively but this measure can be volatile. Therefore, its trend is usually a measure. • Inflation rate and interest rates – If inflation rate is high and interest rate remains low then there is a strong tendency for energy cost to keep escalating.

Sectors	Drivers / Indicators
Financial (XLF) – investment management companies, banks, mortgage services, real estate services, brokerages, etc.	• GDP growth – increasing GDP means the economy is doing well, it would mean less bad loans, increasing interest income and investment income for banks. When stock market is doing well, brokerages and investment management companies perform better as well.

• Interest rates – if interest rates increase, the profits of banks tend to increase while profits of real estate and higher leveraged companies tend to decrease. However, when interest rates are too high, it will negatively affect economic growth.

• Inflation rate – reasonable inflation rate is good for economy in general as it encourages people to spend and companies to invest. However, if inflation rate gets out of hand, then government will enact measures to reign in on inflation such as cutting money supply, reduce credit, increase taxes and interest rates. As a result, financial sector tends to do poorly when inflation rate is very high.

• Change in fixed asset investments – increase in fixed asset investments will lead to increase in loans and improved

Sectors	Drivers / Indicators

asset valuations. Hence, resulting in improved results for financial institutions.

- Existing and new home sales – increase in sales of existing and new homes will generate more income for banks, mortgage brokers, real estate agents etc.

- Real estate prices – real estate is often the largest investment as well as the largest liability of consumers. Increasing real estate prices will make consumers feel more well-off in general and spur more investments and spending. It also encourages businesses to invest in real estate. Real estate companies, REITs, banks and mortgage companies will do well in such a circumstance. Declining real estate prices usually mean higher loan default rates and declining real estate investments which is bad for the financial sector.

- Unemployment rate – Consumer loan default rate is likely to increase if unemployment rate increases beyond a healthy level. If unemployment rate remains high for long periods of time, business and consumer spending is likely

Sectors	Drivers / Indicators
	to remain low or erratic.
	• Regulatory issues – after the 2008 financial crisis, financial institutions come under increasing regulatory pressures that might have negative impact on their bottom lines. It pays to pay close attention to new regulations affecting the financial sector.
Healthcare (XLV) - health care equipment and supplies, health care providers and services, biotechnology, and pharmaceuticals industries	• Demographics – aging population drives healthcare demand. • Regulations – as the healthcare sector is highly regulated, it can be easily affected by new regulations. For example, the recently passed healthcare reform aims to drive down healthcare costs for most people. However, the jury is still out on how this will play out. • Wage growth – increase in wages means more people can afford to pay increasing healthcare insurance premiums and seek better treatment. In the US, one of the indicators used to measure wage growth is the Employment Cost Index. • Development of new technologies – drug, medical equipment and biotechnology

Sectors	Drivers / Indicators
	new developments could benefit the sector as a whole.
Industrial (XLI) - aerospace and defense, building products, construction and engineering, electrical equipment, conglomerates, machinery, commercial services and supplies, air freight and logistics, airlines, marine, road and rail, and transportation infrastructure companies	• GDP growth – economic growth will spur demand for industrial products and services such as real estate construction, machinery and freight services. • Fixed assets growth – usually in the depth of recession, the government will increase investments in fixed assets such as defense and infrastructure projects. As such, industrial sector is usually one of the first sectors that will emerge from recession. • Foreign exchange rates – Industrial companies that depended a lot on exports or foreign income will do well if the domestic currency such as US dollar depreciates against foreign currencies. Firstly, domestically produced goods will be cheaper than its foreign customers. Secondly, foreign income will be higher when translated back to domestic currency. • Change in durable goods orders – a key measure of future manufacturing activity as orders are likely to translate into actual

Sectors	Drivers / Indicators

activities.

- Purchasing Managers Index (PMI) – it is a very important measure of manufacturing outlook as it measures various components such as new orders, manufacturing production, employment, supplier deliveries and inventories. A figure below 50 means the manufacturing sector is contracting and above 50 means it is growing. In the US, it is published separately by ISM and National Association of Purchasing Managers, Chicago affiliate.

- Baltic Dry Index – this measures the price of shipping raw materials and it is usually a leading indicator because raw materials are needed for manufacturing and the fact that investors can check on this index daily means it is a very useful measure.

- Housing Starts and Building Permits – the US has only suffered a recession since the end of World War II when this indicator is pointing upwards. The cause of the most recent financial crisis stems from overheated real estate market in the USA. Pay close attention to the trend of this

Sectors	Drivers / Indicators
	indicator rather than its absolute value as it might fluctuate wildly from month to month.
	• Producer Price Index ("PPI") – it measures materials inflation. As materials cost is an important component of industrial products companies, any significant increase in PPI might have significant negative impact on this sector because their costs increases. Besides, increasing PPI is highly likely to translate into increasing CPI when producers pass on price increases to consumers.
	• Interest rates – most industrial companies are leveraged and customers that buy their products also depend on loans. Thus increases in interest rates tend to impact their results quite significantly.
Materials (XLB) - chemicals, construction materials, containers and packaging, metals and mining, and	• GDP growth –growth in large economic bodies such as US, East Asia and EU drive material consumption. • Fixed assets investment growth – large scale government investments in infrastructure drive demand in materials.

Sectors	Drivers / Indicators
paper and forest products, etc are covered.	• Material prices – increases in material prices will general increase in the profits of the sector as a whole.

• Baltic Dry Index – it tracks the cost of shipping raw materials. An increase in this index likely reflects strong demand for raw materials. Raw materials companies are likely to perform well if this index is trending upwards strongly.

• Foreign exchange rate – Materials prices might increase if US dollar, which prices of most basic materials are denominated in, weakens.

• Interest rates – large increases in materials prices might increase inflation to the point that interest rates have to increase. When interest rates increase significantly compared to recent historical norms and inflation, one has to be cautious about the performance of materials sector as its downstream customers are very sensitive to increases in interest rates as well.

Sectors	Drivers / Indicators
Technology (XLK) - internet software and service companies, IT consulting services, semiconductor equipment and products, computers and peripherals, diversified telecommunication services and wireless telecommunication services	• GDP growth – a growing economy will make corporations more willing to invest in technology, resulting in increases in revenue and profits for many technology companies that serve corporate market segment. Consumers are also more willing to spend on technology products and services when the economy is expanding. • Wage growth – with higher disposable income, consumers are more likely to purchase the latest technological gadgets. Wage growth will also encourage corporations to invest in technologies that will help improve productivity so that productivity growth can keep pace or exceed wage growth. • New technological breakthroughs – Corporations are always looking for the new technological products and services to help increase productivity. While consumers seek new technologies to improve their lifestyles. • Productivity – when productivity growth is slower than labor cost increment, then it might spur corporations to invest in new technologies to increase productivity.

Sectors	Drivers / Indicators
Utilities (XLU) - water and electrical power and natural gas distribution industries	• Population growth – the larger the population, the higher the demand for water, electricity and gas. • GDP growth – growing economy usually translates to higher demand for water, electricity and gas. • Crude oil, coal and gas prices – increase in raw material prices usually have negative impact on utilities as they might not be able to pass on all cost increases to consumers and consumers might also reduce demand if the costs increase too much. • Interest rates – utility companies usually have significant leverage. Hence, higher interest rates will reduce their profits.

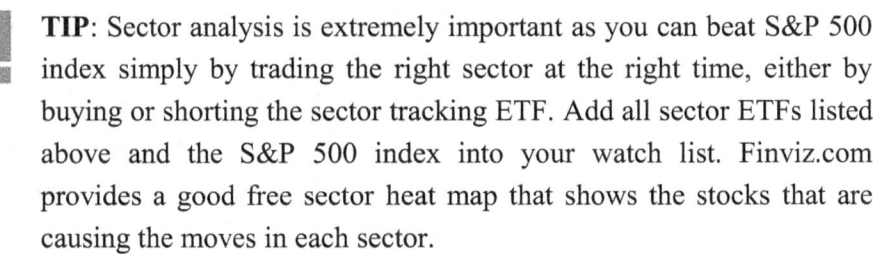

TIP: Sector analysis is extremely important as you can beat S&P 500 index simply by trading the right sector at the right time, either by buying or shorting the sector tracking ETF. Add all sector ETFs listed above and the S&P 500 index into your watch list. Finviz.com provides a good free sector heat map that shows the stocks that are causing the moves in each sector.

Financial Analysis & Valuation

Financial analysis is particularly important when you want to analyze a particular stock. A few key elements of financial analysis will be introduced here. If a company does not pass your financial analysis criteria, it would be unwise to buy its shares for the long term unless it is showing concrete signs of improvements. You can visit Finviz.com, Google Finance and Yahoo Finance to get some excellent free financial information on these companies.

1. **Increasing and positive Operating Cash Flow ("CFO")** – the company must exhibit its ability to consistently increase its operating cash flow in line with its profits as it means good working capital management. Companies that are profitable but have consistent negative operating cash flow have expanded too fast or exhibit poor working capital management. Such a situation cannot last long without the company getting into trouble.

2. **Consistently positive Free Cash Flow ("FCF")** – free cash flow is broadly defined as operating cash flow minus capital expenditures ("capex"). Free cash flow is important as it is ultimately the cash left over for those who have invested in the company. A company that has positive operating cash flow but negative or low free cash flow means it might have spent a lot on capex. One has to scrutinize such investing cash flows rigorously in such cases and understand if the capex can generate higher future returns for shareholders. Furthermore, a business model that requires such heavy investments so that the company has consistent low or negative free cash flows might not have a good and optimal business model.

3. **Consistent revenue growth** – take a look at the company's competitors and determine if its revenue growth is better or worse than them. Read up on the industry and sector to determine if its prospects are good. A company that has declining revenue trend usually will suffer in the form of declining Earnings Per Share ("EPS") growth over time. However, if steps are taken to address declining revenue growth trend then you should determine if these steps taken are effective.

4. **Consistent EPS growth** – Like it or not, EPS is what many analysts and investors look at even though it is a controversial figure. EPS or Earnings Per Share simply means the earnings attributable to each share in the company. If profits increase but the number of shares issued increased proportionately more, then EPS will drop. Hence, it will penalize companies that keep issuing new shares to fuel growth when such new issues are not EPS accretive. A company that has exhibits strong consistent EPS growth is thus an attractive proposition.

5. **High Return on Equity ("ROE")** – Typically calculated by taking profits attributable to shareholders divided by average book value of equity. Compare ROE of a company with its competitors as different industries will have different average ROE. However, one has to be careful as ROE can be boosted by taking on more debt. ROE has strong correlation to Price to Book ("PB") ratio which is an important valuation measure. Higher ROE will usually result in higher PB ratio, all other things being equal.

6. **High Return on Capital ("ROC")** – Some call it return on invested capital, all refers to the same thing. To determine ROC, first calculate Net Operating Profit After Tax ("NOPAT") which is operating profit before interest after accounting for corresponding

taxes. Then divide NOPAT by the average capital employed by the company which will include debt plus net debt of the company. ROC is less prone to manipulation because management cannot change leverage to get higher ROC. Compare ROC of the company with that of its comparable peers to determine if it has done well. Note that ROC might not be a suitable measure for banks.

7. **Strong liquidity position** – Common measures of liquidity include quick ratio and current ratio. Quick ratio refers to current assets minus inventory divided by current liabilities and it is a more stringent measure of liquidity. However, you need to compare liquidity ratio with that of comparable peers as different industries tend to have different norms. A company that is in weak liquidity position coupled by high leverage and low profits or significant losses is usually a recipe for disaster.

8. **Reasonable leverage** – Leverage is a double edged sword. Reasonable leverage will help boost ROE as the company can use the cash from loans to invest in projects that give higher returns. However, excess leverage often spells trouble. You need to understand whether the company can service its loan repayments from the cash generated or it needs to keep "rolling" the loan. The latter practice can be dangerous in the time of credit crisis. A highly leveraged company that does not have a history of strong free cash flow will usually face trouble when things do not go smoothly.

9. **Sound capital management** – Look at the section under financing cash flow in the Cash Flow Statements to understand how the company finance its capital needs or it is returning capital to lenders and shareholders. A company that consistently looks to the

capital markets for more money is not our favorite unless its expected EPS and Free Cash Flow justifies it with ever higher returns per share.

10. **Attractive valuation** – Most important of all, we need to synthesize the information which we with have and form an opinion if the shares of a company are attractively valued. You can have a great company but its shares are overpriced, or you can have a mediocre company but it is trading far below its intrinsic value. Which one will you buy? And which one will you short?

Valuation is a huge topic in itself. For most traders, comparing the Price to Earnings ("P/E"), Enterprise Value to Earnings Before Interest, Tax, Depreciation and Amortization ("EV/EBITDA") and Price to Book ("P/B") of the company against its comparable peers will give a good sense if the company is attractively valued against its peers. Of course there are many other factors to consider such as growth rates, profit margin etc before you can decide whether your company of interest can justify its valuation multiple. Furthermore, you would want to compare its current valuation multiples against its historical valuation multiples.

TIP: If the company has lower valuation multiples than its comparable peers **and** historical average valuation multiples, try to find **strong** reasons that justify such lower valuation multiples, be it slower growth, legal issues, management problems etc. If you cannot find strong reasons that the company is trading at lower multiples then you might have a good buying opportunity. Always give yourself a margin of safety.

There are many books that you can read regarding fundamental analysis but the above factors are extremely important. Hence, pay close attention to them.

TIP: A stock that has high ROE but low P/B ratio compared to its peers might be attractively valued. Screen for stocks with ROE above 15% but P/B ratio below 1 will help uncover some gems. However, take note of intangible assets of the company. High intangible assets as proportion to tangible assets usually increase the volatility of a stock relative to its peers in economic downturn.

Basics of Technical Analysis

There are thousands of technical analysis patterns and indicators and more are constantly being created. However, this book will cover some of the most popular indicators and patterns that are useful to spot and understand trends.

Understanding the rationale

Technical analysis is the study of price charts and the use of information given by price charts to predict the likely future price movements of a particular security. Technical analysis is useful because a lot of people practice it. If it is only you or me who practices technical analysis then it might not be that useful but if a lot of people are using the same signals to place orders then it becomes much more accurate.

The principles of technical analysis are:

- Everything is in the price;
- Price movements are not always random; and

- Price changes are caused by the imbalance between supply and demand of the particular security.

Learn how to read Candlestick

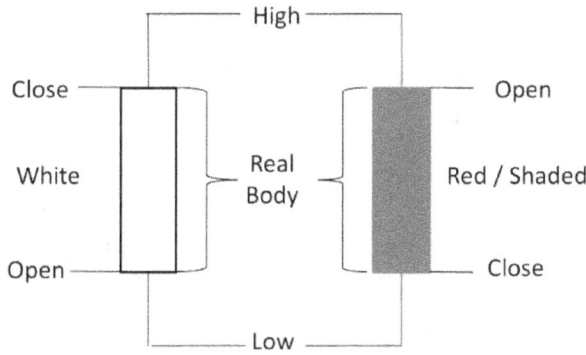

Figure 4-1: Candlesticks

The white candlestick is shown in a candlestick chart when the open is lower than the close at the particular interval of the candlestick. The red or dark shaded candlestick is shown when the closing price is lower than the opening price. Note that a red candle does not mean the closing price is lower than the previous candlestick closing price. In some charting software, the candlesticks might appear in other colors.

Learning the basics

Moving Average ("MA")

- **Explanation**: Simply the average price of previous number of periods. For example, 20-day moving average is the average closing price of the previous 20 days.

Moving average is a lagging indicator as it takes into account the averages of previous closing prices. As such, the longer the period you choose, the less sensitive is the moving average to the most recent price movement.

- **Use**: Using MA helps to smooth out erratic price movements and enable chartists to be able to spot a trend more easily. As it is a lagging indicator, it is often used with other indicators.

Crossovers between two moving averages, such as 9-day MA crossing above or below 20-day MA, can be used trading signals.

Some traders use MA line as support or resistance of a stock price.

- **Effectiveness**: Moving average is most effective if the prices of the security exhibit a trending pattern. Moving average is not effective in tight range bound situations as it will give many wrong signals.

TIP: You might want to use two different set of moving averages for entry and exit signal. For example, enter buy order when 9-day moving average crosses above 20-day moving average and exit your position when 5-day moving average crosses below 20-day moving average as the latter is more sensitive. The rationale is that you want to exit a position more quickly than entering it.

Stochastic Oscillators

- **Explanation**: The stochastic oscillator indicates the momentum of a particular security and it attempts to show buying and selling pressure. The Stochastic oscillator has the %K line and %D line.

The slow stochastic oscillator is perhaps more appropriate oscillator used for trend trading. Hence, it will be explained here.

%K line shows you how much energy the stock price has relative to its trading range over past N periods. %K formula is:

%K = X-period moving average of (100 x (closing price – lowest low over N periods) / (trading range over N periods)

%D line is the Y-period moving average of %K line. Hence it will react slower than %K line. A popular value for Y is 3 periods.

In most software applications, the slow stochastic parameters are given as (N, X, Y) and a popular parameter is (14, 3, 3).

%K and %D line will only have values between 0% and 100%.

- **Use**: Stochastic oscillators are used to spot changes in short term trends quickly. For example some people will buy when %K line cross above %D line and %K line is above a certain value such as 30%. Some will sell if %K line crosses below %D line and %D line drops below 60. For medium term trend traders, you might want to wait for a day after the slow stochastic oscillator gives you a trade signal and also use other indicators to confirm the trend before putting in the order.

- **Effectiveness**: Slow stochastic oscillator is more effective for range bound trading and not as effective for trending stocks. Hence, it should not be used as a sole indicator for trend trading. However, it is especially useful when combined with other indicators and chart patterns.

RSI

- **Explanation**: Relative Strength Index ("RSI") is a momentum technical indicator. RSI is the ratio of average up moves to the average down moves over a period, 9 and 14 periods are popular choices. A rising RSI shows that the stock's upwards momentum is increasing while a declining RSI means the downwards momentum of the stock is increasing. RSI's minimum value is 0% and maximum value is 100%.

- **Uses**: When the RSI is at or above 70% level, the security is considered overbought. Hence, it is riskier to buy into a security that has RSI above 70%. When the RSI hits 30% or below, the security is considered oversold. Hence it is riskier to sell when the RSI hits below 30%.

  A divergence between the price and RSI is a warning sign that the price trend might be coming to an end. A bearish divergence means the price has reached new high but the RSI did not hit a new high. While a bullish divergence means the price has reached a new low but the RSI did not hit a new low.

  Effectiveness: RSI is useful in spotting the beginning and tail end of trends when used in conjunction with other indicators. Use RSI more as a "confirming indicator", for example you might not want to buy with its RSI reading in the overbought region.

MACD

- **Explanation**: MACD stands for Moving Average Convergence and Divergence and it has two lines.

Typically the MACD Line is the difference between 26-period Exponential Moving Average ("EMA") and 12-period EMA. The Signal Line is the 9-period EMA of the MACD Line. The MACD line is the more sensitive of the two lines.

MACD histogram is the difference between the MACD Line and the Signal Line and their difference oscillates around zero.

- **Uses**: MACD is a trend following momentum indicator. For example, swing traders may buy or sell a security when the MACD histogram crosses zero. However for position or trend traders, they might only enter a long position when MACD line is above zero and MACD line is above the Signal line and vice versa for a short position.

- **Effectiveness**: MACD is often used with other trading signals such as divergence pattern between MACD and the price chart can be a rather powerful trading signal. Divergence for a long position means the price of a security has made a new low but the MACD line did not achieve a new low, signaling that perhaps a downward trend is losing momentum.

On Balance Volume ("OBV")

- **Explanation**: On Balance Volume adds a period's volume when the close is up and subtracts the period's volume when the close is down. The OBV line is formed from the cumulative total of the volume additions and subtractions. (Refer to figure 4-2 below)

- **Uses**: The OBV line can be used to compare with the price chart of the underlying security to look for divergences or confirmation. It can be used to signal breakouts and weakening trends if the OBV line diverges from the price chart.

- **Effectiveness:** The OBV line can be a leading indicator of impending trend changes especially when medium term and long term trend changes. It is not advisable to use OBV line to signal very short term trades.

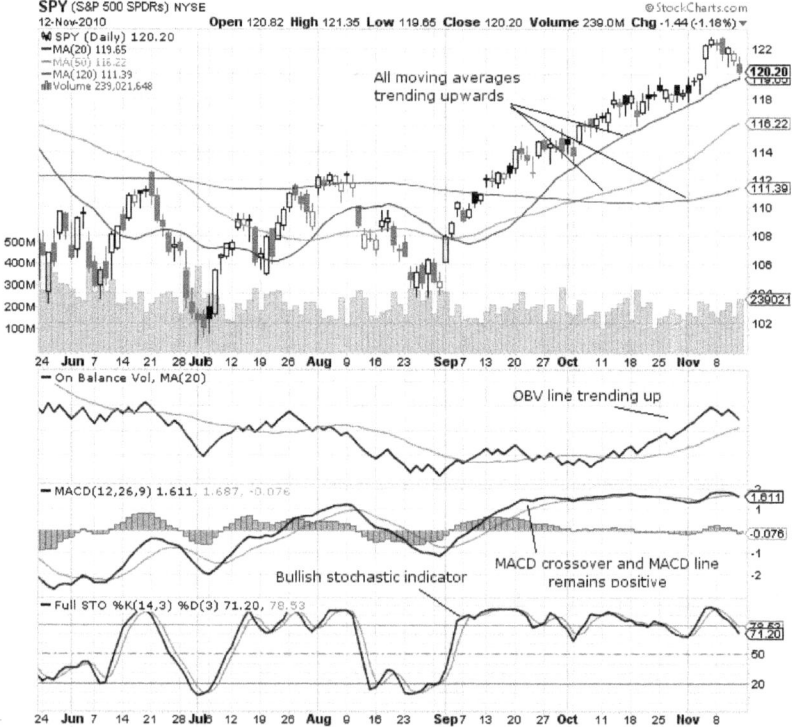

Figure 4-2: OBV, Slow Stochastic Oscillator and MACD

Referring to Figure 4-2 which is the S&P 500 Trust Series ETF ("SPY") price chart, you can see a clear uptrend with all the moving averages and OBV line trending upwards, slow stochastic reached "overbought" level and MACD line remained positive.

Resistance

- **Explanation**: Resistance is typically an upper price level that a particular security has tried unsuccessfully to break out of. It can be a flat straight line indicating a range bound security or a resistance support line of a trending security. (Refer to Figure 4-3)

- **Uses**: It is often used to indicate whether it is the start of a new upward trend or the end of a downward trend. Orders are often placed just above resistance level.

- **Effectiveness**: Resistance is useful when used with other indicators such as moving average and oscillators. There must also be fundamental reasons to break out of resistance level else it might be a weak breakout.

Support

- **Explanation**: Support is a lower price level that a particular security has tried unsuccessfully to fall below. Again, this can be a flat line for a range bound security or a support trend line for a trending security. (Refer to figure 4-3 below).

- **Uses**: Support is often used to indicate whether it is a start of a new downward trend or end of an upward trend. Orders are often placed just below the support level.

- **Effectiveness**: Support is useful to spot end of upward trend and beginning of downward trend. The longer the range bound period is, it is usually convincing when the support is broken. Breaking of support level should be analyzed together with fundamental analysis and other technical indicators.

Figure 4-3 shows SPY trended strongly upwards as it broke price resistance at about $112. OBV, MACD and Stochastic all indicated strong bullish trend.

Figure 4-3: SPY breaks out from resistance and stays above 20-day moving average

Basic trend identifying techniques

Technical analysis helps you to determine whether a trend has formed.

Uptrend (Medium to long term trends)	• Higher intermittent highs, new lows do not fall below previous lows. • Price stays above upward trend line. • If price is consistently above 100-day or 120-day MA and 100-day MA is moving up, it indicates a strong upward trend. However, this is not a hard rule as the number of days might need to be adjusted for different securities. The steeper the gradient of the upward trend, the more bullish is the sentiment.
Downtrend	• Lower intermittent lows, new highs do not raise above previous highs • Price stays below downward trend line. • If price remains below 75-day MA consistently, it indicates a strong downward trend. Notice that 75 days is used here as the gradient of a bearish trend tends to be steeper than a bullish trend. The steeper the gradient of the downward trend, the more bearish the market is.

Basic trend transition identification techniques

Identifying trend transition as early as possible would mean more profits and perhaps less losses. If you suspect a trend is changing against you, the best thing you can do is to tighten your stop loss or exit completely. It cannot be over emphasized that the most important part for trend trading is proper risk management.

Below is the description of technical indicators for bullish transition (bear to bull) using MA as the primary indicator:

- Price closes above an earlier important resistance price when the earlier dominant trend is bearish
- Price closes above 50-day MA
- Price is above 20-day MA and 20-day MA has crossed above 50-day moving average
- For stronger signal, wait for 50-day MA to start making new highs and other indicators also support the transition such as OBV line trending upwards.

Below is the description of technical indicators for bearish transition (bull to bear) using MA as the primary indicator:

- Price closes below an earlier important support price when the earlier dominant trend if bullish
- Price closes below 50-day MA
- Price is below 20-day MA and 20-day MA has crossed below 50-day MA
- For stronger signal, have other indicators confirm the down trend. For example, MACD line crosses below zero.

Breakouts

A breakout happens when the price of a security breaks out of a trading range, be it a resistance or support level. Breakouts are extremely important in trend trading as you do not want to trade a security that is range bound because trading of range bound securities are more suitable for experienced short term traders.

TIP: To determine if a breakout can be sustained, use fundamental analysis to determine the reasons for the new trend to continue. In addition, stock prices often retest a break out from support or resistance. Do not be fooled by the retest. Figure 4-4 shows SPY retested the earlier support at about $120 before continuing with its down trend.

Figure 4-4: SPY retest previous support before it continues its downwards movement

Two Powerful Patterns

It is important that you learn to recognize a few basic patterns. Of course the popular patterns are easily recognized by most traders out there so they often do pan out as predicted. Hence your performance will be greatly improved if you can recognize them.

Double Top

Double Top is formed when the price reached a new high, retreated and then challenged the last new high again but failed. Figure 4-5 shows Microsoft ("MSFT") first reached a new high of $34.71 in early November 2007 before retreating. It attempted to break the last high again near the end of December 2007 but its attempt failed as it reached a peak of $34.41, forming a double top.

Double Top usually signals the end of a bullish trend so be prepared for an upcoming bearish trend. Double tops can be further confirmed by other technical indicators such as MACD and OBV. Double Top can be a very powerful bearish signal.

"Dead cat bounce" is a term used to describe a false hope bullish rally in an attempt to break the bearish down trend. A failed rally in such a case is a strong signal that the stock price will continue its downward movement as evidenced in the example below. MSFT tried to breach $30 but failed and retreated soon after to below $25.

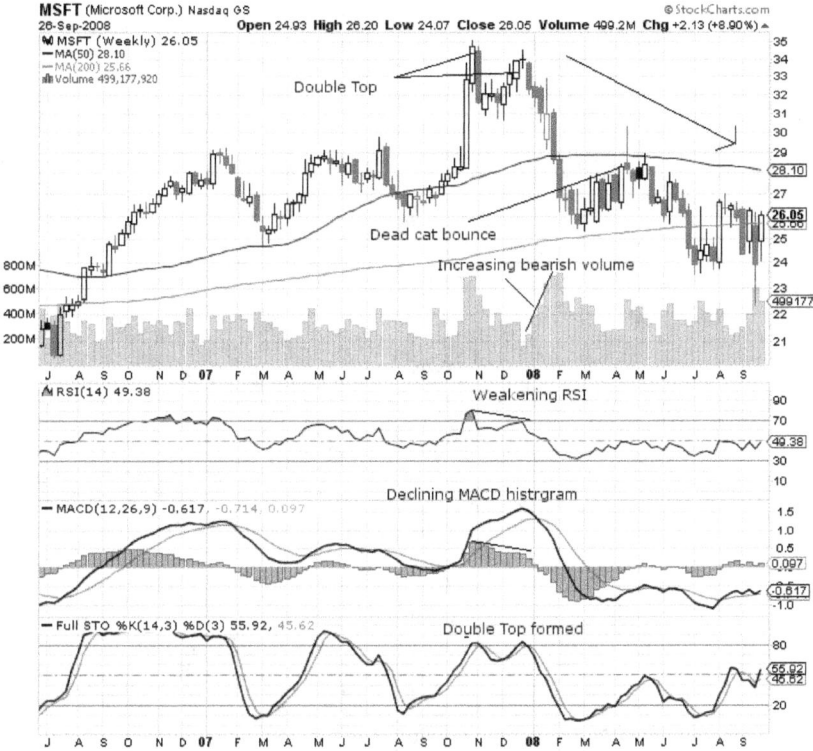

Figure 4-5 Double Top

Double Bottom

Double Bottom is formed when a price formed a new low before rebounding and then it attempted to test the previous low but failed. Double Bottom is the exact opposite of Double Top in that it is a bullish pattern. If the subsequent bullish trend is supported by the market in general, then the rebound will be even more convincing.

Figure 4-6 shows Dell made a double bottom in middle of March 2009 at about $8. After that, it made a bullish run all the way to $14, a gain of about 75% in 3 months.

Figure 4-6 Double Bottom

The Wait

Some traders cannot wait to get into action every day, some every minute of the day. Well, it really depends on your personality. Whatever your style of trading, it is best to wait for high probability signals that meet your pre-set criteria before putting in a trade.

On the other hand, some people tend to hesitate when it is time to pull the trigger and then they see the prices run away from them. Don't despair. There is always another chance to enter.

TIP: Do not chase a trend that has gotten away from you, for example a fixed percentage above your intended entry price, as it often will end badly for you. It is better to search for another stock that gives you better risk reward ratio.

Crossing the road is a good analogy for trading. You wait for the traffic signal to tell you it is safe to cross the road. If the road is very wide and the traffic signal, indicates that you should hasten your pace in crossing the road, would you still cross the road when you have not done so or wait for the next chance to do so? Stock prices are even more dangerous than road traffic as they do not care if you are safe before they move. Will you still attempt to place the trade when not all conditions are met? If the answer is "yes", save yourself some money and do not be a trader.

TIP: Treat your trading capital as the number one asset that you need to protect. To minimize overtrading and reckless trading, try to limit yourself to a low number of trades per week or per day. A possible limit could be 5 trades per week. If you use up the number of trades within the timeframe that you set, you cannot trade any more.

Putting it all together

Figure 4-7 Strong bullish trend with signs at strain near the end

Figure 4-7 shows SPY started another medium term strong bullish trend from August 2006 which was supported by:

- OBV line which is trending upwards from late August 2006;
- 20-day and 50-day MA that are trending upwards since mid-August and it is joined by 120-day MA in early September.
- SPY continued to make higher lows since August 2006.
- SPY stayed above 20-day MA on most days.
- MACD line crossed above zero in early August 2006 and continued its strong upwards trend.

Weakening bullish trend

However, the bullish trend showed signs of weakness as early as mid-November 2006 when MACD line started a clear downtrend.

The weakening bullish trend was confirmed when Stochastic made a lower high in January 2007 despite price movement continued to new high. OBV line also leveled off in January 2007 despite new highs in price.

With 3 indicators showing slowing a bullish trend, a trend trader can consider taking profits in January 2007. SPY indeed slumped on 27 February 2007.

Uptrend continuation

However, a double bottom was formed in March 2007 and it was confirmed by Stochastic and OBV line divergence before making new upward movement which ended with slumps in July 2007.

Action list for Step 4

1. Practice, practice, practice. There can be no substitute for experience. The quickest way to learn is from real world examples. Start monitoring the market index, selected ETFs and sectors.

2. Find someone to mentor you. It will save you a lot of time and money.

   Names of mentor(s): _____

   _____

3. Continue to read various books on fundamental and technical analysis as what was covered here is just the foundation for you to continue your pursuit of knowledge in these areas.

   Books that I have read in the past:

   _____

   _____

   _____

   Books that I am reading or just read:

   _____

   _____

   _____

4. Test yourself with the stock charts at the end of the chapter and determine whether the stock prices trended up, down or sideways after last day shown on the charts. If you can get at least 4 out of 5 questions correct then you are ready to begin trend trading, else please revise the material again. The answers are provided at the end of the book.

   My score: ___ out of 5

   You may refer to *www.trendtradingsignalsystem.com* for more practice questions.

5. Bookmark the home pages of various fundamental and technical analysis websites. Familiarize yourself with the websites that you have selected. A few popular free websites are listed below:

   - **Google Finance** – for detailed stock information and industry peers comparisons
   - **Yahoo Finance** – for excellent free interactive charts and stock screeners
   - **Financial Visualizations** – for stock overview, sector maps and stock screener.
   - **Marketwatch** – for breaking news
   - **Bloomberg** – for Baltic Dry Index, news and other indicators
   - **Stockcharts** – for free stock charts

Test questions (Answers found at the end of the book)

Chart 1

Chart 2

Chart 3

Chart 4

Chart 5

Notes for Step 4

_____

_____

_____

_____

_____

_____

_____

_____

_____

_____

_____

_____

_____

Step 5 – Master different order types

Before you can start trend trading, you need to understand the different basic order types that you can use to enter and exit positions effectively. There are also extremely important for risk management.

Understanding Bid and Ask

You will see bid and ask prices on any electronic trading platform. The explanations below aim to clarify the different quotes that you will get on a typical online trading platform.

- **Bid price** – the price that dealers are bidding for your shares if you are selling shares to them. Bid price is usually lower than the ask price of a stock except in cases of rare market volatility.

- **Ask price** – the price that dealers are asking for their shares if you are buying shares from them. Ask price is usually higher than bid price of a stock.

- **Spread** – the difference between ask price and bid price.

A word of caution - you should trade outside of market hours sparingly and you must always specify a limit price that you will sell or buy a stock outside of market hours because of thin volume and wide spread.

Devise effective order entry and exit strategies

Enter position   Try to use limit orders to enter a trading position whenever possible but my suggestion is that if the price begins to move away from you then quickly enter the trade by using market order. However, if the price moves away from you too much then you might want to consider giving up this trade.

Exit position   Try to set stop limit order or trailing stop limit order beforehand so they are triggered automatically when your exit price is met. In emergency, you can consider using market orders to exit your position.

TIP: Do not place a trade just before or after a big announcement as the market usually takes some time to adjust itself to the news. You should wait for the price volatility to lessen before placing a trade and that usually happens more than 15 minutes after an important announcement. If the price moves away from the target entry or exit price then you may not want to place any trades. Remember this – we don't have to be the first to get into a trade.

Long and short positions

A long position means you own the particular stock. A short position means you have sold a particular stock that you do not have. To enter a short position, you simply sell a stock that you do not own. Short selling will be covered in greater detail here since most people know how to buy stocks but less people understand short selling. However, to be a good trend trader so that you can greatly outperform the buy-and-hold investors, you have to master short selling. With short selling skill in your arsenal, you can make money whether the market is bullish, bearish or range bound.

Selling short is actually quite simple. Say if you sell a stock short at $100 and it later drops to $90 when you buy back the stock, you pocket a profit of $10.

However, the mechanics behind a short sale is a bit more complicated. Basically to enter into a short sale, you need to ensure that your broker can help you borrow the number of shares that you are shorting. In most circumstances, your brokerage should be able to locate the necessary shares for borrowing as it usually keeps an inventory of shares for borrowing. The settlement date for most stock markets is three days which means your broker will borrow the shares to settle your short sales on the morning of the third trading day. There might be net borrowing costs associated with short selling. You have to check with your broker on this.

If your short sale order is small relative to the stock's daily trade volume then you usually will have no problems borrowing the required shares for your short sale trade. The whole process is rather transparent to you. The worst case scenario if you are not able to borrow the required number shares for your short sale trade, then your broker will have to conduct a forced repurchase or "buy-in" at current market ask price and the resulting buy trade will be charged to the your account, thereby reducing or eliminating the short position.

Hence, it is always prudent to check whether a particular stock can be shorted and the number of shares that are available for borrowing before you place any short trades.

For the US stock markets, there is also a new regulation enacted on 10 November 2010 that placed certain restrictions on short selling when a given stock is experiencing significant downward price pressure. This amendment, referred to as the alternative uptick rule (Rule 201) introduces a circuit breaker which takes effect whenever the primary listing market declares that a stock has declined 10% or more from the prior day's closing price. Once the circuit breaker has been triggered, a price restriction is imposed which prohibits the display or execution of a short sale transaction if the order price is at or below the current national best bid.

In this case, assuming Microsoft's ("MSFT") share price was $10 prior to today's open and its bid price went down to $8.90 and ask price is $8.92 after open. Then all short sells order below $8.90 will not be displayed.

Besides when the market is very bearish, such as during the 2008 financial crisis, regulators may ban short selling for many stocks for a limited period of time. This could create huge short covering pressure, i.e. short sellers buying stocks to cover their positions, resulting in upwards movement of stock prices. However, such price appreciation might be temporary in nature if the fundamentals of the economy continue to deteriorate.

Another important point to note is that short sellers do not receive dividends from the stocks that they have sold short. On top of it, short sellers have to pay the dividends in lieu to the persons that lent them the shares.

Options are extremely useful financial instrument for short selling but trading options is beyond the scope of this book. You should become a successful trend trader in stocks and ETFs first before dabbling in options trading.

Although short selling is slightly more complicated than buying stocks but once you master it, you will have a powerful weapon to make money in practically all kinds of market conditions.

TIP: Stock prices usually fall faster than when they rise. Hence, it is important to react more quickly to take advantage of short selling opportunities. However, you also need to manage your risk carefully and be ready to bank in the profits once your trend trading system advises you to do so. Try not to hold on to short positions for too long.

Common order types

There are many different types of orders. Various common order types are explained below using SPDR S&P 500 ETF as example.

ETF	Bid Price	Ask Price
SPDR S&P 500 ETF (SPY)	$100.10	$100.11

Order Type	Explanation	Example
Market order	A market order tells your broker to buy or sell at the current ask or bid prices respectively.	• A market buy order means SPY will be bought at the ask price of $100.11. • A market sell order means SPY will be sold at $100.10.

Order Type	Explanation	Example
Limit order	You need to state the limit price which is the highest price that your broker will buy or sell your stock at. Limit order can be used to control your entry and exit prices.	• A limit buy order with limit price at $100.05 means SPY will only be bought if ask price drops equals or below $100.05. • A limit sell order with limit price at $111.00 means SPY will be sold when its bid price reaches $111 and above.
Stop order	You state the stop price that you want your broker to execute your trade as a market order (typically to exit a position) when the price moves beyond the stop price.	• For long position, you will typically enter the stop price below the current bid price, i.e. *below* $100.10. • For short position, you will typically enter the stop price above the current ask price, i.e. *above* $100.11

Order Type	Explanation	Example
Stop limit order	You state the stop price and limit price such that your broker will execute your trade once the stop price is reached but within your limit price target. Your order will not be executed once the bid/ask price is beyond the limit price. Hence, use limit stop orders with caution.	• For long position, a possible stop price is $99 and the limit price is $98. This tells your broker to sell the stock when bid price falls to $99 or below. However, the stock will not be sold once the bid price falls below $98. • For short position, a possible stop price is $111 and the limit price is $111.50. This tells your broker to buy back the stock when ask price reaches $111 and above. However, the stock will not be bought if the ask price goes above $111.50.

Order Type	Explanation	Example
Trailing stop limit order	A trailing stop limit order allows you to specify a limit on the maximum possible loss. A sell trailing stop limit moves with the market price, and continually recalculates the stop trigger price at a fixed amount below the market price, based on "trailing" amount that you set. The limit order price is also continually recalculated based on the limit offset. Trailing stop limit order is useful for profit protection.	• Using the above example, suppose that you set the maximum possible loss for a long position to $1 and the limit offset is $0.50. If the bid price drops below $109.10 ($1 below $110.10), the market order will be triggered. If the bid price drops below $108.60 ($109.10 - $0.50), this order will not be executed. • If the bid price has increased to $111 then the trailing stop price will increase to $110. If the bid price drops to $110.50 later, the stop price will still remain at $110, i.e. $1 below the highest bid price reached. • The reverse is true for Buy trailing stop limit order.

Examples of Effective Entry and Exits

The two examples described below are for short and medium term traders. However the concept is the same regardless of your style.

Effective buy orders

Figure 5-1 shows two different long position entry orders, one for the short term trend trader and the other for the more conservative medium term trend trader that thrives on breakouts and do not like to trade in a range.

The earlier buy order at about $107 would be entered on 1 September 2010 based on the following signals with the intention to sell at $112 if the breakout fails:

1. MACD histogram, Stochastic and RSI divergence as they failed to make lows when price made new low
2. Price bouncing off a strong support at about $104

A short term trader might take profit when profit target is met and net $5 per share for this trade.

Another buy order would be entered on 24 September 2010 at about $114 when the retest of the resistance at $112 failed. At that point in time, the moving averages and other technical indicators all support bullish trend. The Federal Reserve then had hinted of quantitative easing to boost the economy. US dollar also began to weaken against most major currencies, boosting hopes of US exports increase and fueling commodity prices increase.

Figure 5-1 SPY Buy Orders

Effective buy and short sell orders

In the next example shown in Figure 5-2, a buy order is entered on 16 February 2010 at about $109 with the support of the following signals:

- MACD, Stochastic and RSI divergence as they failed to make new lows when price made new low
- 5-day moving average crossed above 10-day moving average
- Price moved above 20-day moving average
- Belief that euro zone debt issues could be contained

- Signs of economic recovery

A sell order was entered on 27 April 2010 to take profit at about $119 when on the close of 26 April 2010, netting a profit of about $10 per share in this trade. The following take profit sell signals were generated:

- RSI and Stochastic divergence as they failed to make new highs when price achieved new high
- MACD histogram lacked momentum in the bullish trend
- Opened next day at below 10-day moving average
- Goldman Sachs was indicted and Greek crisis became more serious

A short sell order is generated near the close of 30 April 2010 at about $119 when:

- 5-day MA crossed below 20-day MA
- 10-day MA turned downwards
- Slow Stochastic %D line fell below 50
- RSI was trending down
- Bearish engulfing candlestick appeared
- Fear caused by euro's future and cuts in EU spending
- Indictment of Goldman Sachs drove financials down
- Fear of double dip recession gaining traction

A trailing stop buy order was triggered on 11 June 2010 to close out the short sell order at $109, again netting about $10 per share in profit, when the following technical indicators supported the trade:

- RSI and MACD divergence
- Price closed above 20-day MA line

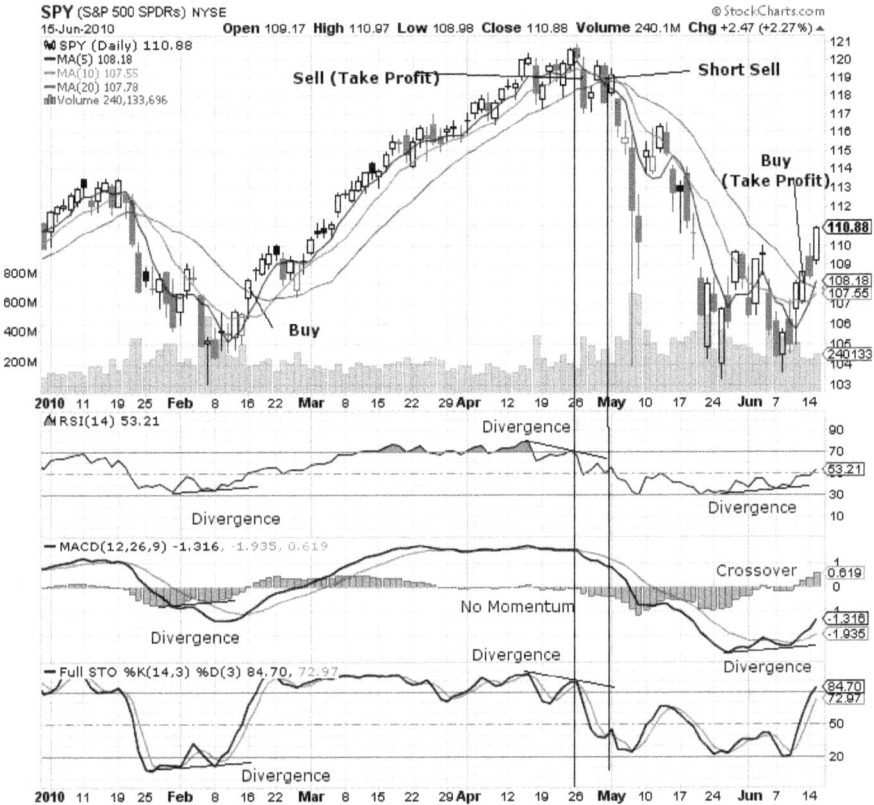

Figure 5-2 SPY long and short orders

Volatility

What is volatility?

Price variation is measured by volatility in trading. Volatility is referred to as standard deviation of a security's price by some while others term it as variance of a security's price. In any case, standard deviation is simply the square root of variance. What is more important is what to do with increasing or decreasing volatility.

In most cases, increasing volatility is usually caused by price slumps and vice versa. Hence, if you spot an increasing volatility in a security that you are trading, you should trade with more caution.

Volatility tends to cycle between high and low as a security goes through bullish and bearish trends. Traders keep an eye on volatility to adjust their trading plans for that particular security.

It is mentioned in Step 4 that one should monitor the volatility index of S&P 500 or VIX as it is often referred to as the "fear gauge". The higher the reading, the more fear there is in the market.

High volatility means the trading is generally riskier as price swings are large. However, the chance for profit in such a situation is also greater. On the other hand, low volatility is less risky for traders but the profit potential over a short period of time is also lesser.

TIP: Swing traders will usually trade stocks with higher volatility than position traders or longer term trend traders. However, it is just a matter of preference. If your risk appetite is low, then you should not trade high volatility stocks. Don't be influenced by others that you must trade either low or high volatility securities. Make up your own mind from your trading experience.

Some illiquid stocks exhibit very high intraday price volatility that could easily trigger your stop loss orders. Hence, if you plan to trade volatile and illiquid securities, it is advisable to give a larger allowance for the high volatility.

How to know a security's volatility

You can easily obtain a stock's volatility from Financial Visualizations (Finviz.com) website or other financial websites.

Another way is use the security's historical beta as a proxy for its volatility as beta can be obtained from Google Finance or other financial websites.

Beta is used to describe whether a security moves in line with the market, e.g. S&P 500, as a whole. A positive beta means the security generally will move in the same direction as the market and a negative beta means the security will move in the opposite direction of the market. A beta that is greater than one or less than 1 means the security's price will tend to move in the direction with or against the market in a more volatile manner.

Hence, you can assume that a stock with higher beta is generally more volatile relative to the market than a stock with a smaller beta value. However, beta is at best a proxy of relative volatility and not a measure of volatility itself. Hence, beta will not detect the market is becoming more or less volatile. But assuming if you know the market's volatility from VIX, you can draw rough conclusions about a stock's volatility based on its beta.

TIP: One important thing to note about volatility is that it can change rapidly depending on the general market news and that of the market. Hence, projecting future volatility based on historical volatility can be a dangerous business. It is best use as a guide for setting your stop loss and also confirming the general direction of the market.

Uses of volatility

You might want to screen out securities whose volatility is below or above your comfort level. As mentioned earlier, some traders prefer to trade securities with high volatility, others prefer low volatility securities.

A security's volatility will determine how you set your stop loss and trading indicators. As a general rule, a volatile security should have larger stop loss allowance. Furthermore, you can lengthen the period of your technical indicators, e.g. use 9-day MA instead of 5-day MA.

Trading on margins

Although trading on margins can increase your profits significantly, it can magnify your losses even more rapidly. Hence, use margins with care. You should check with your brokerage regarding the margin interests and fees involved for margin trading and the rules governing its use.

TIP: Remember that if the equity value of your account falls below the minimum maintenance margin, you will receive a margin call from your broker asking you to deposit additional funds in your account. If you fail to deposit the required additional funds into your account in time, the broker will liquidate some or all your trading positions. At times, your broker might even liquidate some of your trading positions before there is any margin call if it is likely that the margin call will be triggered.

You should try margin trading until you have significant trading experience under your belt. Try margin trading only after you have gone through one bull and bear cycle. If you come out on top after a complete cycle, then you might consider margin trading. Remember that you can lose more than what you have with margin trading.

Action List for Step 5

1. Make sure you understand the different order types and you can experiment with it through simulated trading and then with minimal trade capital. Strike out the order types below that you have tested. You should try these order types for "Buy" and "Sell" orders using a demo/practice account.

   A. Market Order (Buy / Sell)
   B. Limit Order (Buy / Sell)
   C. Stop Order (Buy / Sell)
   D. Stop Limit Order (Buy / Sell)
   E. Trailing Stop Order (Buy / Sell)
   F. Trailing Stop Limit Order (Buy / Sell)

2. Decide which order types work for your trading style. It should be noted that your preferred order types do not mean you won't use your non-preferred order types. Always set stop loss orders for all positions.

   My preferred order types are:

   A. _____
   B. _____
   C. _____

3. Go to Finviz.com and select SPY. Take note of its volatility, average true range ("ATR") and beta. Do the same for the symbols XLP ("Consumer Discretionary Sector Select SPDR") and WDC ("Western Digital"). Observe the price movements of XLP and WDC over three days in relation to SPY by paying special attention to their price volatility.

Notes for Step 5

_____

_____

_____

_____

_____

_____

_____

_____

_____

_____

_____

_____

_____

_____

Step 6 – Develop your trend trading strategy and system

Now that you have learnt about your trading style, risk appetite, fundamental analysis, technical analysis and different order types, you are ready to develop your own trend trading system.

Developing your own trend trading strategy and system is critical if you want to be successful. You must adhere strictly to your trading strategy and system. In the next step, you will learn how to systematically fine tune them as you trade.

What is a trend trading system?

Your trading system should consist of your collection of fundamental and technical analysis criteria woven together to generate buy and sell signals that suit your trading style and objectives.

Ultimately, you want to develop a trading system that you are comfortable with. For example, you might not like to trade too often and prefer to trade major trends then you might want to develop a trading system that consists of longer term fundamental analysis and technical analysis indicators.

TIP: The importance of technical analysis increases as your holding period shortens.

Whether you use a mechanical system in which a trading software will enter trades for you once you set the rules or you use a discretionary system in which you will enter trades yourself, you need to make sure the system is robust and suits your personality and risk appetite.

Steps to develop strategy and system

1) For most traders, your trading strategy and system should cover what you are going to do when you are faced with these seven scenarios: -

   a) Bullish transition – security turning from bearish to bullish trend

   b) Bullish trend – persistent raising trend

   c) Bullish pullback – a correction or pull back while the general bullish trend is still intact

   d) Bearish transition – security turning from bullish to bearish trend

   e) Bearish trend – persistent downtrend

   f) Bearish pullback – a correction while the bearish trend is still intact

   g) Range bound – the price of a security is trading within a tight range

2) If you are starting out, you should focus on bullish and bearish trends. The scenarios are just to prepare you for these two trends.

3) Decide on your ruling concept. Do you want to trade every small trend or you are only interested in the primary trend? Whether you call it momentum trading, swing trading or position trading, a trader only makes money if the position he is holding goes up or

down sufficiently for him to make a profit. The ruling concept is usually determined by the length of time you are willing to hold a position and your risk appetite.

4) Set your fundamental and technical screens for BULLISH and BEARISH trends.

5) Develop a proper risk management system and make sure you have clear entry and exit points before you trade.

TIP: Many novice traders started out without having a clear exit strategy. As a result, many of them suffered huge losses because the more losses they suffered the more they are unwilling to exit their positions. Hence, never let a small loss turn into a big loss.

6) Develop a checklist that you will check off before you make any trade. The concept is that you will only enter positions in securities that your checklist approves. Hence, your checklist is important for making sure that you analyze all relevant factors in detail before entering a trade. A good checklist should make sure you consider whether the following support your trade:

- Fundamental analysis
- Technical analysis
- Probability
- Risk Reward Ratio

You can check out a sample trade checklist from our website.

7) Keep a trade journal that consists of at least the following fields.
- Date of Trade

- Symbol
- Stock Name
- Type of Trade – buy or sell
- Entry Price
- Stop Loss Price
- Profit Target Price
- Actual Exit Price
- Number of shares/contracts bought
- Total Amount Bought
- Profit/Loss Amount
- Profit/Loss Percentage
- Reasons for Entering Trade
- Reasons for Exiting Trade
- Post Trade Analysis

You can use a notebook or a spreadsheet to keep the journal. You can download a sample journal from our website.

8) Review your checklists, trade journal, strategy and system after sometime to fine tune them. For example if you find that you make the right bets but you still did not hit your profit targets because you hold your positions too long then you can consider tightening your profit target or trailing stop price so that you bank in your profits as soon as possible.

Selection

Tools for Screening

There are many free screening tools available out there to help you screen for stocks that meet certain fundamental criteria that you want.

Some of the free screening tools out there for the US markets at the time of writing that you can consider are (not in any ranking order):

- Yahoo Finance – provides excellent web based and java applet based screening tool. The java applet based screening tool has more features for more advanced screening.

- Google Finance – the great thing about Google Finance is that it lists out the comparable stocks of a company you are researching on the same page. Hence, it makes it much faster for you to compare valuation and other fundamental metrics. If you are interested in a specific industry or in multiple industries, you will certainly find this to be extremely helpful way to screen stocks based on peer comparison.

- Financial Visualizations (Finviz) – provides good set of fundamental and technical screening tools that are easy to use even for a novice. The great thing about Finviz is that it allows the user to match a complex set of technical and fundamental criteria unlike other free screening tools that is strong only in either technical or fundamental analysis.

- Stockcharts.com – has a suite of free pre-set scans. It is useful for those who trade on certain simple technical patterns. If you require more complex technical screens, then you can subscribe for its paid service which is not that expensive.

- FreeStockCharts.com – provides a good technical screening tool for those that sign up as free members. The charts are also customizable which are extremely useful. You can even add screened stocks to your portfolio.

- Your online discount broker – many online brokers provide excellent free screeners nowadays. This is definitely the first stop for you when you search for good screeners. In fact, it should be one of your key criteria when you select a online brokerage. Make sure that your chosen broker provides the right tools to help you succeed.

- Screens based on third party recommendations – There are dozens of free websites that tout that they can give you free stock picks. Check whether their methodologies suit your trading style. They can be an useful source of trading ideas but you need to carefully analyze each trading tip yourself before making any trading decisions.

TIP: There is not one free tool mentioned above that can meet all the needs of a serious trend trader. Hence, you need to know which tool to use to obtain the information that you seek. The best tool could be provided by your online broker.

Setting fundamental screening criteria

One of the strongest correlations between performance of companies and valuation metrics can be found in the relationship between Return On Equity ("ROE") and P/B ratio. Although I will not go into their mathematical relationship here but it is mathematically proven that a company with higher ROE should result in higher P/B ratio.

This concept can be easily explained using an example. The book value here refers to the book value of equity. Say Company X with equity of $100 that had an annual return of $50 meant Company X had a ROE of 50% ($50/$100 x 100%). At the end of the year, its book value or equity will be $150.

Say Company Y also had equity of $100 but it only provided an annual return of $10. Therefore, Company Y had a ROE of 10% and a book value of $110 at the end of the year.

If Company X continued to add $50 to its book value at the end of each year compared to Company Y which was adding only $10 to its book value annually then it made sense that Company X should be priced at a higher P/B ratio compared to Company Y.

A good way to find undervalued companies is to use a new ratio that I termed as the Book Value Return Ratio (or simply PB-ROE ratio which some may call it) which is derived from dividing P/B by ROE. If a company has higher Book Value Return Ratio when compared to its peers or the market in general then it is likely that the company is overvalued base on the ROE it has achieved.

TIP: To find undervalued stocks, you consider screening stocks with Book Value Return Ratio that is below 1. This is only one of the many criteria that will be applied but it is a useful one as ROE and P/B are readily available and the Book Value Return Ratio can be easily calculated.

Step 4 mentioned several fundamental analysis criteria that you must take note off. For quick screening, you can use Price/CFO ratio which simply takes the current market capitalization of the company divided by its operating cash flow. Then eliminate those companies whose P/CFO ratio is much higher than P/E ratio because high quality earnings must be supported by strong operating cash flows. Besides, there are enough companies in the stock market universe so you want to focus on those that have been generating cash from operations.

Next, focus on companies that consistently churn out positive Free Cash Flows or FCF. If you recall my earlier definition of FCF is CFO minus capex. A company that has high CFO but negative FCF over a period of years means its internal cash generating capacity is not sufficient to support its growth. Then there are only two ways left for it to raise capital, by issuing more shares or taking on more debt. If the company is already highly leveraged then the only way out is to issue more shares and that is likely to dilute future EPS if the company is not able to generate high returns on equity.

Of course the next important criteria to consider would be the P/E ratio. A high P/E ratio might not be a bad thing but it really depends on your investment style. A company with high P/E ratio is frequently supported by high P/B ratio so Book Value Return ratio screen usually eliminates those with the highest P/E ratios.

Depending on your risk appetite and trading style, some trend traders like to trade cyclical stocks, others prefer non-cyclical stocks. It is really a matter of trading preferences. For trend traders, trading cyclical stocks can be an extremely profitable venture but if you are new to the game, it can be quite risky as well.

To spot cyclical companies, you can look at their historical EPS and projected EPS since cyclical companies' EPS will have obvious peaks and troughs. If you go under the financial statements section of Google Finance or Yahoo Finance, you should be able to find historical EPS data quite easily. Finviz provides consensus estimate of future EPS. If the EPS of a stock is going down in the next quarter or next year then the stock most likely is going through a down cycle.

TIP: An important thing to note is the declining EPS does not mean declining stock prices. Remember that that stock prices adjust to future expectations very quickly. Hence, you need to use other measures to make sure the stock is undervalued before concluding whether the stock is under or overvalued.

Setting technical screening criteria

A good trend trader never gets into position when the stock is not trending. Hence, while fundamental criteria are highly important in supporting your trading decision, technical analysis tells you when to enter and exit your position.

The **Rule of Three** simply states that you only get into a trade when at least 3 of the technical indicators in your system agree with your trading decision. This means that one needs to have at least 3 technical indicators in your trading system.

Pattern recognition trading, such as spotting double top, cup and handle, ascending triangles etc, is usually more difficult for novice trend traders to spot accurately. Hence pattern recognition should be used to support your technical indicators and not used as a primary signal.

The easiest technical signal to use will be **moving average crossovers**. That is a faster moving average line, say 9-day moving average, crossing above or below a slower moving average line, say 20-day moving average.

A slightly slower but usually quite accurate technical indicator is the direction of a very slow moving average line such as the 80-day or 120-day moving average line. For example, a buy signal can be generated when 80-day moving average line changes from flat or down trend to up trend. A sell signal can be generated when 80-day moving average line changes from flat or up trend to down trend. Do note that if you do use this signal as mentioned above, it is usually meant for medium to long term trend traders.

Another easy to use technical indicator is the **OBV line**. A raising OBV line should support your buy decision while a declining OBV line will support a sell decision. OBV line can be used as a leading indicator at times. For example, if a stock price continued slump is not supported by declining OBV then it might signal that the stock might make a direction change soon.

A commonly used oscillator is the **MACD** as this useful lagging indicator can be used to detect divergence between price movements and the strength of the price movements as mentioned in Step 4.

The next commonly used indicator is the **Slow Stochastic Oscillator**. You can use this screen to find stocks that are either overbought or oversold. If the %D line is above 80 then the stock's upward momentum is strong and the stock is likely to be overbought. On the other hand, if the %D line is below 20, then the stock is likely to be oversold. Crossovers between %K and %D line can also be used.

TIP: Usually %K and %D line can stay in overbought or oversold territory for weeks if the trend is extremely strong. A good entry and exit point is when %D line enters 45 to 55 range. If the trend is persistent then %D line will continue upwards or downwards. Hence, you can screen for stocks with %D line between 40 to 60. You may use %K line instead of %D line as your primary signal line, it really depends on your preference.

There are many other technical indicators out there. However, the above technical indicators should suffice most of the time. In any case, you do not need to trade in every situation. You just need to trade when you are really convinced that a trend has started.

Which one first?

Some traders wonder whether fundamental screen should be applied before technical screen or vice versa. Of course, if you can apply both screens at the same time will be ideal.

Building your own trend trading system means you have to experiment with a system that suits your skills and personality. Some people do not like fundamental analysis at all and rely totally on technical analysis. It works for some trend traders but it can be dangerous unless you are really quick witted and experienced.

If you are new to trend trading, it will be wise to pick a set of stocks and ETFs and understand their fundamentals really well so that you do not need to spend too much time analyzing their fundamentals when the technical indicators signal you to trade.

You can do really well trading the index, stocks in your chosen sector or industry because you have more time to understand their fundamentals and price behavior.

Therefore, you shall not deviate from your initial chosen set of stocks and ETFs till you are successful for at least 3 months.

Choice of stocks and ETFs to trade

If you are starting out in trend trading, you may want to consider choosing SPY and the Sector Select SPDRs that I mentioned in Step 4 to trade. These are highly liquid counters and they are not as easily influenced by large block traders than less liquid counters.

For example technology sector ETF tracks the Nasdaq index quite closely so it is a good proxy for Nasdaq as well.

TIP: You can obtain fundamental information on SPY and Sector Select SPDRs from these securities' official website. You can check out their valuation multiples, holdings, beta past performance etc from the respective securities' fact sheet.

If you want to include some stocks in your initial watch list, you can consider picking one stock with the best fundamentals and one stock with the worst fundamentals from each sector to complement your sector trend trading strategy. The stock with strong fundamentals is for long trades and the one with weak fundamentals is for short trades.

TIP: Do not touch leveraged ETFs unless you are day trading or you know exactly how the ETFs behave with regards to holding them for long periods. Some of these leveraged ETFs are not meant for medium or long term trading.

Rules of Risk Management

Risk management is often overlooked aspect for new traders. However, this is perhaps the most important aspect of trading. Below are ten rules of risk management that you should remember and practice.

Fast And Simple Steps To Profit From Trend Trading

1) Only place trades that meet your criteria;

2) Only trade when the risk reward ratio, which is calculated by dividing expected profit by expected loss, is favorable. For example, you may want the risk reward ratio to be above 2.5 times, i.e. you are likely to make $25 profit for risking $10;

3) Capital protection should be your top priority because without capital, you are out of trading business;

4) Never let a big profit turn into a small profit;

5) Try not to let a small profit turn into a loss;

6) Never let a small loss turn into a big loss;

7) Never trade against the dominant trend;

8) Make sure you analyze the probability that you are right and wrong;

9) Make sure you consider the volatility of the security that you are trading and whether you can stomach its price volatility;

10) Never over leverage as that can wipe you out before you have the chance to learn; and

11) Don't over diversify because if you have too many open positions, it will be very difficult for you to track all their movements and trading costs will be high.

As a rule of thumb, you should not have more than 3 open positions when you first started out because you need more time to get used to monitor these positions. Do not commit all your trading capital till you become reasonably satisfied with your results in trend trending.

TIP: Consider trend trading ETFs that has average volume of above 1 million shares a day such as S&P 500 index and the various sector ETFs introduced earlier because they are usually less volatile than most stocks.

Find a mentor or partner

Some people like to trade without any interaction with others. Some do better with others guiding them. For most beginners, you will do much better if you have a mentor or partner that can review your decisions against your trend trading system's trading criteria.

Key reasons that you should find a mentor or partner are because:

1. **Two brains often produce better decisions than one.** Most investment and trading professionals make decisions in teams, especially if they are not the top dog. Professionals understand the benefits of collective wisdom. If professionals need others to review their decisions, then it is even more important for novices to have others to review trade decisions.

2. **Prevents you from getting caught up by emotions.** Most novice trend traders get too emotional when trading and they make irreversible mistakes that were pointed out in this book. It does not matter when you are on a winning streak or losing streak, having a partner or mentor will probably help you remain rational.

3. **Makes you think harder.** You are likely to think more carefully before you make any trading decision if you know others are reviewing it.

4. **Improves your analytical ability.** A good mentor will help to improve your analysis by challenging your justifications for certain trade decisions. Hence, you get to learn from someone who is more experienced.

5. **Helps you to stay motivated.** Trend trading can be emotional for many people even when you are a experienced trend trader. Having someone to share your frustrations and happiness helps you stay motivated in down times and rooted in good times.

6. **Helps to ensure that you follow your system.** A good trusted mentor or partner can help you check your decisions against your trend trading system either before or after you place your orders. This will encourage you to be more disciplined in your trading.

Testing the system

Testing a system can be time consuming but fun especially when you combine both fundamental and technical analysis. You can begin testing your system by noting down your trades on a piece of paper or on the computer to gauge how you perform first.

No matter how good a system is, you need to follow it consistently as it may generate wrong signals a few times before it gives you the right signal and that right signal may just generate huge returns for you. Therefore, give your trading strategy and system a chance to have a proper dry run before changing it.

Action List for Step 6

1. Determine your trading style and time horizon that you will hold each position.

   My trading style: _____

   The time horizon that I intend to hold most positions barring any stop loss being triggered (you can select more than 1 but it is not advisable if you are just starting out):
   A. Less than a day
   B. More than a day but typically less than a week
   C. Between a week to a few months
   D. More than a few months
   E. Never going to sell unless macroeconomic conditions changed drastically – typically for more than a year
   F. Never going to sell regardless of market conditions

   If your answer is (A) then you are a day trader. If your answer is (B) then you are likely to be a swing trader or short term trend trader. If your answer is (C) or (D) then you are a medium term trend trader. If your answer is (E), then you are a long term trend trader. If your answer is (F), then you are not a trader and this book might not be that suitable for you.

2. Select the stocks and ETFs that you want to monitor on a consistent basis. If you are new to trend trading, you should monitor highly liquid and less volatile stocks and ETFs. You can consider starting with SPDR S&P 500 ETF and Sector Select ETFs. Spend some time to monitor them on a daily basis.

Symbols of stocks/ ETFs / other financial instruments that I will monitor on a regular basis (Not more than 25):

_____

_____

_____

3. List the accompanying fundamental analysis indicators for each stock or ETF that you monitor.

   You may use the Notes page at the end of this chapter.

4. Develop the technical analysis signals that you will master and follow. Make sure your trade meets the criteria of at least 3 technical signals that are in your system before you place a trade. You can rank the technical signals. For example, you will only trade if your No.1 (primary) technical indicator is met and confirmed by at least 2 other technical indicators.

   My preferred technical signals are :

   1. _____

   2. _____

   3. _____

   4. _____

   5. _____

5. Develop your own trade checklist that you will use before you make trade. Your check list should consist of the technical indicators and fundamental criteria that you listed in the earlier two steps above. You can group them up as well. For example, you can tick of whether at least 3 technical indicators are met and if fundamentals support your trade decision. You should also include the win probability assessment and Risk/Reward ratio in your check list. A sample is available on the book's website.

_____

_____

_____

_____

6. Determine the stop loss limit formula for each stock that you have selected which is suitable for your risk appetite. Always set a stop loss for every trade. You can consider using a percentage stop loss initially that is equal to 2 to 3 times the Average True Range of the stock or say 3% to 4% from the entry price. As you become more experienced, you can make adjustments to the stop loss base on trading patterns and technical indicators.

Note that you can use different stop loss methodologies for different securities.

My preferred stop loss method(s) are (select more than 1):

A. Percentage loss
B. Fixed price limit loss
C. Trailing percentage or price loss
D. Fixed amount loss
E. Technical indicators or patterns
F. Average true range
G. Beta x Fixed Percentage Loss for stock with Beta 1

Elaborate any stop loss methodologies here:

_____

_____

_____

_____

7. Set your profit targets for each stock. For trend traders that use daily charts, it will be good to set a fixed percentage profit to exit or use a few technical indicators to determine your exit. You can consider using trailing stop limit order as well so you take the emotional aspect out of profit taking.

My preferred method(s) of exiting a trade (other than stop loss being triggered) are (you may state more than 1 method):

_____

_____

_____

8. Start a trade journal. It would be preferable to keep the trade journal in electronic form using a spreadsheet or word editor. A sample is available on the book's website.

9. Find a broker or online brokerage service. There are many cheap online brokers out there such as Interactivebrokers and TD Ameritrade. Interactivebrokers provides you with a rather powerful standalone trading platform for free but this platform is rather sophisticated. If you find its standalone platform too sophisticated, you can try out its web trading platform which has a simpler user interface.

   My online broker is: _____

10. Test your system using historical data and simulate actual trading using live prices by using a demo/practice account before actually applying it to your real account.

Notes for Step 6

Step 7: Review and fine tune your goals and system

In the earlier chapters, the importance of keeping your trade journal up to date was mentioned. Keeping a good journal is especially important if you are just starting out because it will help you improve your trend trading system.

Unless you can devise a trend trading system that is suitable for all conditions and objectives, it is most likely that you will have to review and fine tune your trading system on a regular basis. No one gets it right the first time, so do not be disheartened. The important thing is to know what went right and what went wrong in actual trading.

Besides, a trade journal also allows you to determine whether you are even following your system! Some traders don't follow their systems and then they start blaming their systems do not work! Don't be one of them.

TIP: If you keep forgetting to update your trade journal, then you can set a trade journal entry reminder alarm on your computer or cellular phone so that it reminds you at the end of each trading day. Furthermore, you can even have your mentor or close family member inspect your trading journal. It is not easy to motivate yourself to keep a trade journal so try this method to see if it works for you.

Furthermore, you want to review the goals that you have set for yourself. Ask yourself whether your goals are realistic or they are too ambitious. For example, some traders demand that they achieve 10% return on their portfolio monthly. Sometimes your trend trading system simply is not setup to achieve such returns so you need to adjust your goals accordingly.

Do not deviate from your system

To be able to review and fine tune your system, you must first give your system a chance. It is very easy to deviate from your system as greed and fear might dominate your emotions and thinking. Do not deviate from your system unless you have extremely compelling reasons to do so, such as to cut a loss that you can no longer afford. Never open a new position that does not meet your system's criteria. You have the chance to change your system when you review it.

Do and Don'ts when reviewing your system

- Review your trading system at least at the end of each week when you are first starting out. You can progressively lengthen the time to two weeks or longer when you have a successful system.

- Review all your trades made and NOT made. Look at each trade carefully to determine how you can tweak your system so that you will not make the same mistakes again.

- You can have more than one system when you have sufficient experience so that each system will cater to a particular style or product type. For example one system for swing trading, another system for position trading. Alternatively, one system for trading ETFs and another for trading stocks.

- Take note of the changes you made to your system. Sometimes you will need to partly or completely roll back the changes made.

- Do not keep changing your system unless it is consistently not meeting your expectations. Give your system some time. At times it is not your system that is the problem, it could be the fact that you are not following your system properly.

Action List for Step 7

1. Start placing trades from the trade signals that are generated by your trend trading system. Remember to always start trading with smaller amount of capital until you are confident that your trend trading system works as expected.

2. Set daily reminders on your computer or cellular phone to remind you to update your trade journal at the end of each trading day.

3. Set a weekly reminder on your computer or cellular phone to remind you to review all your past week's trades and fine tune your system. It might be better that you review your trades over the weekend when you have time to cool down.

   Day and time of weekly review is: _____

4. Review your trade journal at the end of each week or whatever frequency you think it is suitable for your level of experience and track record.

   Enter the trading mistakes that you made in the first week of your review here. You should continue to keep a journal of your weekly trade analysis.

Take note of any repeated mistakes and whether you made any of the mistakes that were mentioned under the chapter "10 Common Trend Trading Mistakes To Avoid".

Trading mistakes that I made in the 1st week are:

_____

_____

_____

5. Keep a log of all changes that you made to your trend trading system and take note of the dates that you start implementing the changes. Your log should consist of at least the following entries for each change:

    a. Date of Change
    b. Change Made
    c. Rationale
    d. Implementation Date
    e. Results

6. Compare the back test and actual trading results of your latest trend trading system against the results of the previous version.

7. Use different systems for different product types or trading styles when you have sufficient experience.

Many times, it is the consistent small improvements that you make to your trend trading system that will eventually make you successful. So do keep it up!

Notes for Step 7

10 Common Trend Trading Mistakes to Avoid

If you can avoid the 10 common trend trading mistakes listed below then you should be on the way to becoming a successful trend trader. Remember that in trading, it is usually the mistakes committed that separate a successful trader from an unsuccessful one.

Therefore, memorize the 10 common mistakes listed below if you want to be successful trend trader!

1. Trading against Dominant Trend

Always remember to check the dominant market trend by using the most representative index for that particular stock market, and in the USA, it would be S&P 500 index. If the stock market index is very bullish then try not to short sell any stock or ETF unless you are absolutely convinced that there is an extremely high probability that the stock will continue to crash (note: it is often better to have several indicators supporting your bearish analysis before you attempt to short a stock in a bullish market). It is the same when the stock market is bearish, it would be quite foolish to start buying stocks for a trend trader when the market is still in a nosedive.

2. Not sticking to your Trend Trading System

Many failed trend traders never follow their trend trading system consistently. Hence, when they fail to achieve expected results, they do not know what changes to make to trend trading system. A trend trading system is absolutely necessary if you want to succeed in trend trading as it acts as your guide and prevents you from jumping haphazardly at every opportunity. A person that cannot follow his own system is not serious about trend trading and he will soon find it to be a very costly mistake.

3. *Timing the Tops or Bottoms*

This mistake has to do with trend traders who become impatient or too greedy. They do not wait for their system's signals to confirm entry or exit points and try to beat their own system by entering positions too early or exiting positions too late, only to lose money. Some trend traders cannot take profits even though their indicators tell them to do so, only to see their profits dwindle later. Do not be one of them.

4. *Taking Losses Too Personally*

Many trend traders get extremely emotional when a trade goes against them. It is really silly as they only hurt their own emotional and physical health. Sometimes it even affects those around them. No experienced trend trader ever achieves a 100% track record in making the right trades. Everybody makes mistakes, the trend traders that succeed are those that lose small and win big.

5. *Lack of Patience and Want Quick Results*

Trend trading is not for those that want immediate success. Few people are that talented. You need practical experience of thriving in bullish and bearish market conditions before you can claim to be an accomplished trend trader. Many traders give up after a few bad trades. As pointed out in Step 1, you need to really know why you are getting into trading in the first place.

6. *Chasing a Runaway Trend*

If the price has already gone way beyond your entry price then it might be best to wait for a pullback before entering a trade. It makes sense to give opportunities that ran away a miss as sometimes you might get burnt by pullbacks and retests.

7. *Adding to loss making positions*

Adding on more of your precious capital to a losing trade is the sure way for a trend trader to go out of business very soon. You might get lucky sometimes that the stock goes back in your favor but all it takes is a bad trade to wipe out a large chunk of your trading capital. Adding to loss making positions is also extremely unhealthy to one's emotional state. It is almost always better to cut loss and wait for the stock to start a new trend before entering it again.

8. *Ignoring Your Stops for Profits and Losses*

Some trend traders do not enter stop loss or trailing orders but instead have them written down somewhere, convinced that they will pull the stop loss trigger when the stock actually breached the stop loss price. Unfortunately, not many people can pull the trigger when they see losses. Even if you could be one of those unemotional traders out there, you still could miss the stop loss price that you want.

9. *Too much Diversification*

Some say "Diversification is for birds". While some diversification is good but some trend traders overdo it by having more than 30 open positions for a small account. The trading and monitoring costs are simply too high when you have so many open positions. With the proliferation of ETFs in recent years, you would probably be better of trading a few ETFs if you want so much diversification. Beginners should start with less than 5 "high conviction" positions.

10. *Lack of Consistent Diligence*

There are trend traders who are fair weather friends. They are happy and committed to trend trading when the going is good for them. However, when the market turned against them, they either become ostriches (i.e. refuse to look at their portfolio and watch lists) for fear of knowing or simply get out of all positions and stop trend trading till they hear that their friends are making a killing in the market. Such trend traders are unlikely to succeed in trend trading as success can only be achieved if there is consistent diligence. Remember that hard work does pay off in trend trading. Failure always gives in to those who are persistent.

Final Word

Trend trading is an excellent way for you to make consistent profits in either bull or bear market. As stated in my introduction, this guide book is meant to provide you with step-by-step advice and instructions on how to profit from trend trading. However, your trend trading education does not end with this book.

The exciting and interesting part about trend trading is that you can trade under almost any market condition. Hence, you are always occupied and you have to keep yourself up to date with the latest information, analysis and trading techniques.

There are many sources of information on trend trading or specific financial instruments out there that you will find useful. Hopefully this book has played its part in helping you succeed in trend trading.

You can also join our community of trend traders by visiting our website at *www.trendtradingsignalsystem.com*. On this website, you will find some latest trend trading commentaries and resources that will help to improve your trend trading skills.

Some of the resources that you can find on this website include list of great free information providers, charting software, industry news etc. You also get a chance to contact us regarding any questions that you may have after reading this book.

Do remember that trading is a risky business. Hence, proper risk management separates the winners from the losers.

I wish you will have a fruitful trend trading career!

Answers for Step 4

Chart 1

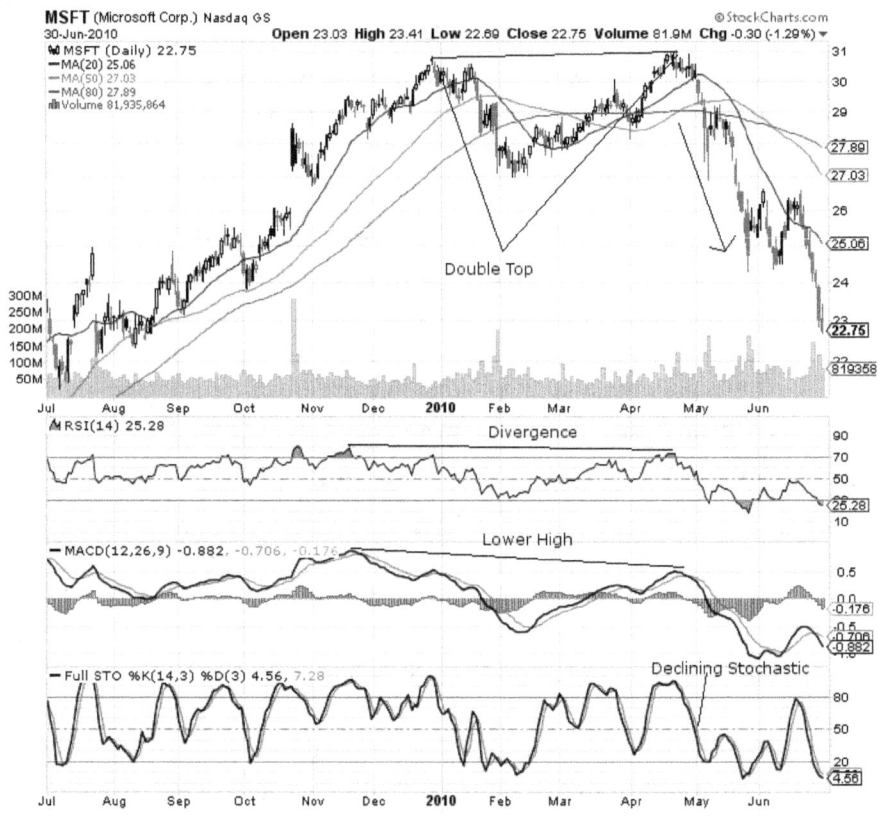

Answer – Down

MSFT moved down after displaying Double Top and it was confirmed by the technical indicators.

Chart 2

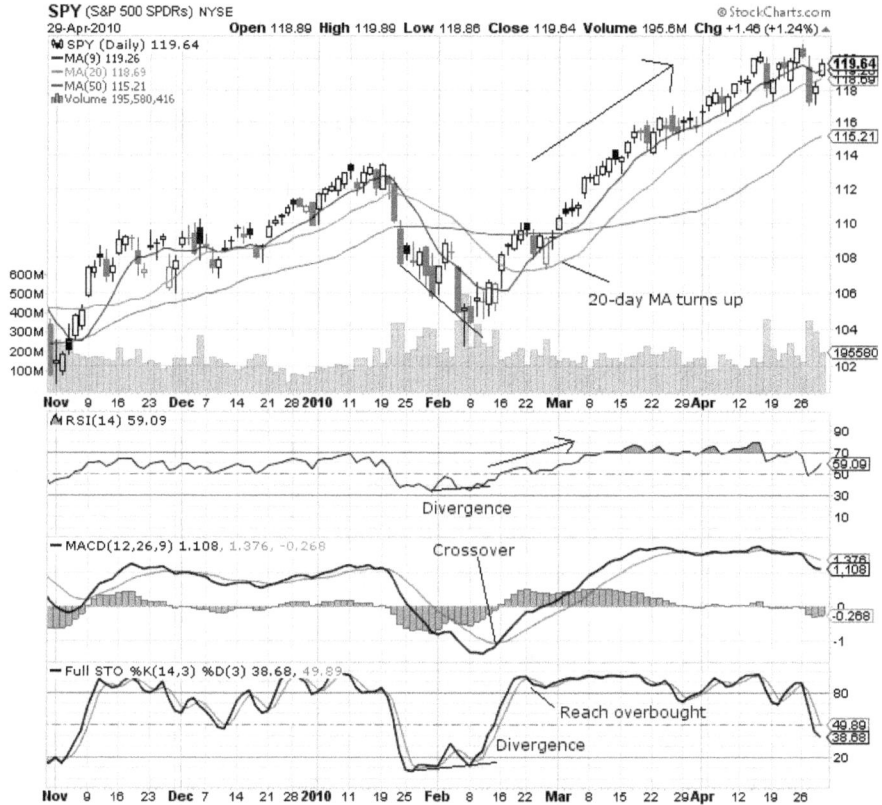

Answer – Up

20-day had moved up. RSI and Stochastic made a higher low despite price reaching lower low. MACD crossover was detected.

Chart 3

Answer – Down

9-day MA line crossed below 20-Day MA line. RSI and Stochastic were moving lower. MACD histogram was negative. Furthermore, there was a very bearish candlestick on 18 Apr 2010 which showed the bulls were beginning to lose grip on the up move.

Chart 4

Answer – Down

XLI made new high on 9 Oct 2007 but RSI, MACD and Stochastic all did not make new highs. Furthermore, price had crossed below 9-day MA and there was a bearish engulfing candlestick on the next day, 10 Oct 2007. All these signals point to a bearish trend forming.

Chart 5

Answer – Up

XLE had reached resistance. However, RSI, MACD line and OBV were all trending upwards, suggesting that the breakout might succeed this time. Furthermore, 50-day MA line was slowly moving upwards.

Index